THE

911

& 912

PORSCHE

**A RESTORER'S GUIDE
TO AUTHENTICITY**

DR. B. JOHNSON

ISBN 0-929758-00-5
Library of Congress Catalog Card Number: 88-90976

Published by Beeman Jorgensen, Inc.
7510 Allisonville Road, Suite 11, Indianapolis, IN 46250 U.S.A.

Printed and bound in the United States of America
Printed by White Arts, Inc., Indianapolis, Indiana
Cover design and photography by Llew Kinst, Sunnyvale, California

For wholesale and bulk distribution information please contact:
The Practice Ring, Inc. Attention: Marketing Director
7510 Allisonville Road, Suite 12, Indianapolis, IN 46250

Second Printing, January 1991

CONTENTS

To my wife Julie and to my parents
for their understanding and support.

ACKNOWLEDGMENTS

Should the reader think that this endeavor was accomplished single handedly, let me dispel those notions. It is hard to express my appreciation for the unselfish contributions and cooperation from the people and organizations listed below.

First, a special thanks to Jay Burgess, parts manager at Giganti Porsche-Audi, Indianapolis, Indiana, for patiently answering countless technical questions as I attempted to translate parts manuals into readable text. His good spirits and cooperative nature made bothering him a true pleasure.

I am also grateful to the following "experts" for supplying informational literature and for proof reading this text for technical accuracy, spelling, grammar etc. (yes, this is the section where I distribute the blame). Without the help of these people, the following text would have been considerably less thorough and correct: Gene Babow, Bruce Baker - *Auto Research Associates,* Frank Barrett - *Toad Hall Motorbooks,* Bill Block - *Block's Books,* Mark Haab, Jerry Keyser, Dick Naze, John Paterek - *Paterek Brothers,* Brad Ripley - *Porsche Cars North America,* Ron Roland, Cole Scrogham, Mick Williams - *Stoddard Imported Cars,* Theresa Wilson and Ted Zombeck.

Without the following photographers and photogenic models, I can assure you that this book would not be particularly useful. It would have been a bit cumbersome to credit each photo, but these are the nice people and their friends:

Ron Roland, New Haven, MI, '64 901 coupe
Bob Fleming, Minneapolis, MN, '64 901 coupe
Roger Schneider, Pittsburgh, PA, '65 911 coupe
Cole Scrogham, Waynesboro, VA, '65 911 coupe
Bill Lovett, Brighton, MI, '65 911 coupe
Woody Chapman, Norwalk, CT, '65 911 coupe
Dick Naze, Muncie, IN, '65 & '66 911 coupes
E.R. Maxfield, Peoria, IL, '66 911 coupe
Tom Scott, Denver, CO, '66 911 coupe
Tom Beauchamp, Noblesville, IN, '66 912 coupe
Orr Potebyna, Seattle WA, '66 912 coupe
Bill Brannan, Decatur, GA, '66 912 coupe
John Markle, Cloumbus, OH, '66 912 coupe
Bill Block, Tupelo, MS, '66 911 coupe
Drew Ivancic, Bradford, PA, '66 911coupe
Doug Rich, Redding, CA, '66 912 coupe
Alan Davis, Columbus, NE, '67 911S coupe
R.T. Broskowski, Sun City, AZ, '67 912 coupe
Ron Keister, Columbia City, IN, '67 912 coupe
Joe Jerdonek, Brecksville, OH. '67 911S Targa
Richard Harris, Louisville, KY, '67 911 Targa
Russ Duclos, Redding, PA, '67 912 Targa
Ted Zombeck, Dublin, OH, '67 911S coupe
Diane Scott, Columbia Station, OH, '68 911L Targa
Bill Grodi, Sun Lakes, AZ, '68 911L Targa
Steve Hahn, Goleta, CA, '68 911S Targa
Jerry Allston, Phoenix, AZ, '68 912 coupe
Sam Wash, Zionsville, IN, '69 911 coupe
Neal & Kathy Lepovetsky, St. Marys, PA, '69 912 coupe
Dave Tidball, Meadow Vista, CA, '69 911T coupe
Stoddard Imported Cars, Willoughby, OH, '70 911S coupe
Dennis Yuro, Edison, NJ, '70 911S coupe
Tom Lekas, Oklahoma City, OK, '70 911T coupe

Wade Miller, Penn City, PA, '71 911T coupe
Bob Gollibur, Woodbury, NJ, '71 911T coupe
Paul Cary, Shreveport, LA, '71 911E coupe
Mark Thompson, Indianapolis, IN, '72 911T coupe
Bob Schmitt, Cockeysville, MD, '72 911S Targa
Stuart West, Peachtree City, GA, '73 911T Targa
John Meyer, Cincinnati, OH, '73 911T Targa
John Fitze-Clarke, Vancouver, BC, '73 911S Targa
Greg Way, Shreveport, LA, '73 911T coupe
Roger Eiteljorg, Indianapolis, IN, '73 911 Carrera RS
Frank Barrett, Lakewood, CO, '73 911 Carrera RS

Finally, I would like to thank Porsche AG for giving their permission to reproduce the illustrations from the 1965 through 1973 Factory parts manuals which are contained in this book.

Brett Johnson

FOREWORD

Brett Johnson and I have been acquainted for approximately twenty years. When we first met at Arlington High School, my job was to teach him the fundamentals of the French language, a task at which I have been fairly successful for a number of years. The two year foreign requirement was the norm in those days, but Brett opted for a three year sequence. It was actually fun to have a room full of eager students who always did the assigned work faithfully and came to class prepared to do battle with the Present Subjunctive and the Plus-que-Parfait. What a contrast with some of the "reluctant learners" that we teachers face in our classrooms today!

The late 1960's and the early 1970's were turbulent times, but somehow, the advanced French class remained an "island of calm and tranquility" among all the rebellion and discontent that certain students demonstrated then. Brett came through it all in fine form, rising above all the turmoil and retaining his own special individualism which serves him even now in his work as a doctor of veterinary medicine and in the off-duty activities which he pursues as a private citizen.

Brett was the only student at school who drove a Porsche. That car was a visible testimony to his ability to rebuild and restore what someone else had discarded. He seemed to take great pride in the inventory of old cars that always cluttered up the family driveway. Now Brett has effectively transferred that talent for rebuilding sports cars to his career in caring for animals as he very skillfully "repairs and gives renewed life" to the fortunate pets that are brought to his office each day.

Brett and I have managed to keep in touch over the years. It is always a pleasure for a teacher to learn that a former student has attained success in his chosen field and is making his contribution to society. The subject matter is not all that important. Values learned and applied in one's daily life are what count.

William S. Fishback

INTRODUCTION

While rummaging through some memorabilia in one of my many junk drawers, I located a photo from my seventh grade class. On it was written "To a fellow Porsche enthusiast" in the best penmanship that John Wharton could muster. While my enthusiasm for the marque goes back a long way, I did not actually own a Porsche until I reached the age of sixteen. The 1957 cabriolet, which set me back $325, confirmed what I had suspected all along: This was my kind of car! But the impetuous nature of youth steered me from the classic Porsche to the power and form of the newer Porsche. I labored many $1.75 hours at my father's animal hospital and parted with my beloved 356A to acquire that Polo Red 1967 911 without engine and gearbox. It was the only Porsche in the Arlington High School parking lot, appearing with a freshly rebuilt 1750cc 356 engine which blew up enroute one morning making me late to health class. In its second incarnation with an engine from a '66 911, which had suffered from an interior fire, its throttle rod stuck making me late to health class yet again. This time I was taken into the hall and given a talking to by Mr. Shambaugh.

While this car (and subsequent ones, as well) seemed to get in the way of my formal education, it continued to fuel my enthusiasm for Porsches. So what if the instruments fell out when accelerating, they were not the original ones anyway. The freshly installed Corvair gas heater definitely out performed the original Porsche heat exchangers. I don't remember what radio I put in, but I am certain it originated in something other than a Porsche. It was with this in mind that I began this endeavor.

Many well meaning former owners have altered their cars, nearly beyond recognition in some cases. Restoring these to their original appearance is often the goal of a new owner and for many, it is not an easy task. Many answers are buried deep within the weighty, burgundy covered parts manuals that grace the shelves at the Porsche dealership. Other answers are seemingly lost to obscurity. While changes to the 900 series Porsches are more systematic than those on the earlier 356 models, there are many unacknowledged differences and running changes. In a number of cases Porsche superseded an original item with a superior piece. The result while frustrating to the restorer was meant to better the marque. I have attempted to bring some of these to light and also to illustrate the original part, where possible.

The purpose of this text is to aid those enthusiasts who have taken the restoration challenge, as well as entertain the Porsche trivia buff. While I am certain that there may be some inaccuracies and uncertainties, I have attempted to put together a complete and accurate description of 1964 through 1973 Porsche 911 and 912 cars. It is my hope that those who can shed additional light on the information that follows would step forward and share it, so that it may be included in subsequent editions. Regardless, I feel that the information within will be helpful to the amateur, as well as the expert. I have tried to depict it in a logical, front to back, system by system, presentation of standard production vehicles. Subject matter is limited to body, chassis, exterior trim, luggage compartment and interior. Reference material is contained in the final section.

I am in debt to those who supplied information and to those who have taken time to review this text for accuracy and to those who have provided photos. In cases where non-original parts are found on photo subjects, I have endeavored to call them to the readers attention.

The first Porsche 911 and 912 models were far from the sophisticated versions produced today, but when compared with their contemporaries they serve as a benchmark for automotive excellence. It is my hope that this book will allow you, the Porsche enthusiast, to better understand the automobile which we both revere.

THE MODELS

This book will examine the non-mechanical aspects of standard production versions of the Porsche 911/912 built between the 1964 and 1973 model years. That is to say, before the coming of the "crash bumper". A subsequent volume will examine the 1974 and later 911. Special production, one-offs etc., have not been included since discussing these would serve little purpose to the average car owner or restorer.

There was only one fundamental change in the period from 1964 to 1973, and that occurred in the 1969 model year with the lengthening of the wheelbase from 2211 mm to 2268 mm. This was not the only change, by any means, that happened during this span of time, as subsequent pages will reveal; however, the terms short wheelbase (SWB) and long wheelbase (LWB) will be used throughout this text and should be referenced to this change.

When put into production in 1964, there was only a single body style, the coupe. For the 1967 model year the Targa, a semi-open version featuring an integral roll bar, was introduced. These two configurations re-mained the only ones for the period covered by this book.

While there were only two body styles, a myriad of engine types combined with varying trim combinations make restoration of the 911 or 912 a bit confusing. While record keeping by the Porsche factory was, all in all, much better than it was in the era of the 356, there are still areas where information is sketchy. There is also some confusion, especially with early models which may be titled or registered a year later than their production year. When in doubt, go by the chassis number. A detailed chassis number list is found on pages 76-83. Throughout this text, the model year will be used to identify cars and features. In most cases the model year commences in late summer or early fall of the preceding calendar year.

A general description of the various models of 911 and 912 is found in the "spotters guide", which makes it possible to identify various years and models at a glance. It can be found on pages 85-89.

Short wheelbase (SWB), 1965-68, coupe and Targa

Long wheelbase (LWB) Targa and Carrera RS

1

Porsche Part Numbers

Those who have ventured into the local Porsche dealership on occasion no are doubt aware of the eleven digit number that identifies each and every component that makes up each car. While somewhat overwhelming by their sheer size, there is a logic to the format. A few general features will help both the novice and the expert.

The first group of three numbers *generally* relates to the car type, engine type or gearbox type. Examples:

901 Early 911 or originally early 911
902 912 or originally 912
905 Sportomatic gearbox and associated hardware
911 Generally, parts added after 1969
915 1972-1973 915 gearbox and associated hardware
925 Late Sportomatic gearbox and associated hardware

There are other numbers scattered throughout, including 904, 914, 916 and 923. These imply origin in the development of other Porsche projects. There are also a few 644s which are holdovers from the venerable 356.

900 and 999 begin part numbers fitting the general classification of hardware, i.e. nuts, bolts etc. It appears that 999 tends to be more of a standard "off the shelf" component, while 900 represents a more specialized part.

Finally, showing that Porsche cannot break away from its humble beginnings, there are occasional nine-digit numbers which may or may not be followed by a letter. These are Volkswagen parts. They commence with numbers such as 022, 111, 113 and 311.

The second group of three in both Porsche and VW part numbers serves to further define the part. For example, in the number 901.559.307.40, which is a "targa" insignia, the 559 is a number which defines insignias and other trim parts such as a 911.559.432.00, which is a right horn grille.

In the part number above, the third group (432) is used to define side. All left side parts end in odd numbers and are generally lower numerically than their right counterpart. Conversely, all right numbers are even and generally higher than their left counterpart. In this case, the corresponding left horn grille is a 911.559.431.00. If the part is not sided, it will be odd.

The final pair of numbers again further defines the part. It was a little clearer cut in the 356 series of numbering: for the most part, 00 represented the first permutation of a part with higher numbers such as 01, 02 etc. being subsequent modifications. Unfortunately, this is not always the case. Using the "targa" script number 901.559.307.40 and its subsequent version 911.559.307.40, we can spot two problems. First the "40". 20 and 40 tend to appear when parts are peculiar to open cars, so the first number was not the fortieth crack at making a "targa" script! The newer script, which differs only by color, is not a 41 but rather shows its revision by alteration of the first group from a 901 to a 911. Sorry, but that's the way it is.

Throughout the text, part numbers will be referenced when it seems appropriate, but not in an attempt to overwhelm the reader nor add to the page count by listing them for each part described.

Tools of the Trade

Aside from actual examples of the marque and a little personal experience, most of the information contained within came from carefully researching the factory parts manuals. The set used consists of the following:

1965-68 911 (originally supplied as a 1966 and a 1967/1968 edition)
1966-68 912 (same as above)
1969-70 911/912
1971 911
1972-73 911

Other relevant factory publications, including color books, sales literature, accessories catalogs and the chassis number chart, round out the reference material.

EXTERIOR BODY PANELS

Bumpers

The original design for the Porsche 911 featured integral bumpers that incorporated the lower valence panels. Actual bumpers did not appear until 1974, when dictated by U.S. crash standards.

The front bumper on the short wheelbase cars was mounted by "L"-shaped brackets much like the 356 models which preceded them. Openings for fog lights had either Hella 128 units in place or were covered by steel covers with rubber seals. As is shown in illustration 8/4 of the 1965-1968 parts book, the first cars with these covers featured a single-bolt mount that attached in the same location as the fog light. According to the parts manuals, this type cover was used up to chassis number 305 100, which corresponds to the hundredth 912 built in 1965. This cover was also fitted to 912s built by Karmann; however, the chassis number for the last car so fitted is not recorded. The 902 part number also flags this as a 912 part. All 911s of this era came with fog lights as standard equipment. The fog light cover plate was changed subsequently to one mounted from the rear by two nuts and a flat bracket. The earlier type cover measured approximately 6 1/2" x 4 1/4", while the later version was larger, 7" x 4 7/8". Since there was no modification to the bumper, these could be retrofitted to earlier cars.

Front bumper 1967 912 showing late type fog light cover

One other interesting bumper-related piece is the ballast that is euphemistically referred to as a bumper reinforcement. These 25-lb. cast-iron dumb-bells were introduced to help out in the handling of the "tail happy" SWB 911. They were fitted as standard equipment on all 1967 and 1968 911 models, but not on the better balanced 912. When they were first installed is not documented, but it was likely mid-1966. These were mounted by wedging them into an existing bracket in

combination with adhesive, making it possible to "update" earlier cars.

Illustration 8/4, 1965-68 Parts Book

1969 through 1973 cars came equipped with a bumper that from outward appearances was virtually identical to the earlier version. Substantial changes were present, though, including a revised mounting arrangement. A much shorter "L"-bracket attached the bumper to the car. The difference in mounting is immediately apparent by looking to the inside of the bumper where the bracket attaches. On the early car the two mounting bolts are in a horizontal arrangement. On the later bumper they are vertical and attached by those annoying 12 point socket-headed screws.

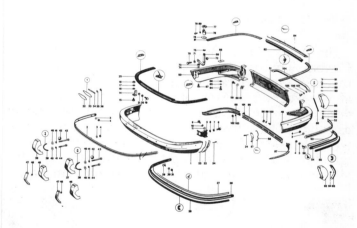

Illustration 8/4, 1969 Parts Book

Fog light openings are again provided, although the bracket to hold the fog light is modified to hold the back-mounting Hella 169 fog light instead of the top-mounting 128. The cover was unchanged on those cars not fitted with fog lights. Finally, the trailing edge of the bumper has an aluminum trim piece riveted in place as opposed to the early model, which does not.

Standard on the 1972 911S and the 1973 911E and S was a modified front bumper with an attractive split chin spoiler. It could be fitted as optional equipment

Early bumper with rolled edge

Late bumper with aluminum trim

on all other models and was constructed from steel. The split in the center was due to the location of the towing hook mounted below.

Split "S" bumper

The final front bumper type was fitted to the 1973 Carrera, which was not supplied to the U.S. market. It retained the general appearance of the "S" spoiler above except that it featured a central box which was designed to contain an oil cooler; although, production cars did not have them mounted in that location. These were also steel. Neither of the last two bumper types could be fitted with fog lights, nor did they have the aluminum trim caps found on the standard bumper.

1973 Carrera RS front bumper

Rear bumpers followed a progression similar to the

front. The SWB body on the 1965 through 1968 911/912 was actually the same length as its LWB replacement. Its rear wheels just were farther from the back of the car. Because of this, the rear bumpers are easily differentiated, early ones being longer.

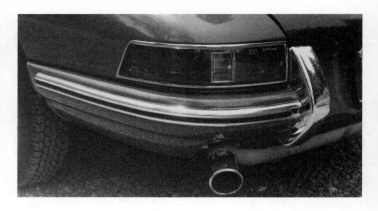

SWB left rear bumper, note cutout for exhaust

The rear bumper on the 911/912 is a three-piece affair. The two outer parts would be mirror images were it not for the cut out in the left side for the exhaust tip. The third piece fits between the outer bumpers and serves as location for mounting the license or registration plate. Since these panels were painted prior to installation on the body, they are finished in living color on both sides.

The sole change to the rear bumper took place when the wheelbase was modified in 1969. Not only was the later version shorter, due to the extension of the wheelbase, but a modification to the leading edge was made. On the SWB bumper this surface was rolled inward and covered with a stainless steel trim piece, while on the LWB style it is cut off flush and covered by an aluminum trim piece.

LWB rear bumper, compare protrusion from fender with SWB version above

Different rear bumpers were found on the Carrera model, because of the slight flare on the rear wheel arch. They were constructed from steel which is noted in the parts book. On racing versions a one-piece plastic rear bumper replaced all three pieces and the trim, including guards. Bumper trim is addressed on pages

Flared rear bumper of the 1973 Carrera RS

18-19 and 33-34.

The center, license plate panel, remained unchanged from 1964 through 1973. It was steel and had depressed areas to lend rigidity. Reinforcement panels were located on the inside surface where the plate mounted. In 1970 and 1971 this panel was aluminum on 911S models. No plate mounting brackets were supplied by the factory.

License panel sans plate

Front Fenders

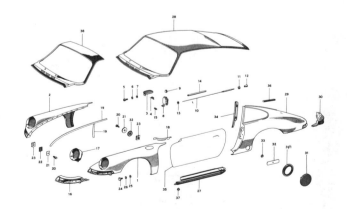

Illustration 8/3, 1965-68 Parts Book

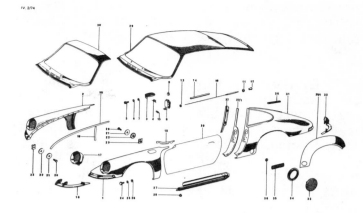

Illustration 8/3, 1971 Parts Book

The SWB 911/912 front fenders were steel and the left side featured a gas filler lid. A change was made in 1968 to accommodate the revised headlight arrangement necessitated by the U.S. regulation prohibiting glass-covered headlights. There was no change in the corresponding non-U.S. cars. The U.S. cars had four brackets located inside the headlight bucket and secured the headlight assembly. No such brackets were found on non-U.S. spec. cars. The change in front fenders is not acknowledged by the parts book nor is the change in fenders that occurred when the horn grilles were modified. This happened during the 1966 model year. This change in the fender consisted of additional brackets by which the two screw grilles were attached. Grilles are discussed on page 20.

Flareless SWB front fender, wheels not authentic   *1968 front fender shows narrowing*

One other unheralded change is the narrowing of the inner lip of the wheel arch. The lip was narrowest at the top of the arch and became gradually wider as it reached the height of the bumper, where it was the widest. The purpose for this tapering was to accommodate the larger 5 1/2" wide wheels introduced in 1968.

The LWB cars had a totally new stamping with new accentuated fender arches. Recognition of the difference between the U.S. and the rest of the world is made in the parts books from 1969 through 1973. The only difference is headlight brackets as mentioned above. One other change between the old and the new was a modification of the box which holds the horn grille and turn signal. The SWB version has a completely enclosed box in which the turn signal resides. The LWB version is totally open with a strip running along the bottom only.

Early Porsche-built body with "sandpaper" texture

Late hood with PVC type sound deadening

Upper latch mechanism and VW bump stops

Front hinge with pneumatic strut

LWB front fender with small flare

Hood

Here's an easy one. No official changes were made from 1965-'73 making all hoods interchangeable. There are some subtle differences not acknowledged by the parts manuals. In 1972 and 1973, the left side luggage compartment light receptacle was no longer present. Also, the inner surface, inside the structural framework, had a textured sound deadening material. This was a sand paper rough asphalt material on SWB 911 and 912s with Porsche built bodies. Karmann built SWB bodies and all LWB cars had a PVC material similar to the the coating on the underbody.

Hinges were unaltered. Borrowed from the VW parts bin were two screw-in rubber bump stops and keeping the water from entering the luggage compartment was a perimeter seal made of foam rubber. The hood was supported in open position by a pair of pneumatic struts attached to the hinges. The struts mount with the thick part at the top (closer to hood) and the shaft end down.

The latch mechanism, which was cable operated from

the interior, featured a double latch, which would release when squeezed. The lower part of the latch incorporates a very clever system which releases not only when the cable is pulled, but also when the cable breaks, thus eliminating the need for access holes necessary on 356 models. This latch mechanism was used on all models from 1965 through 1973.

Front lower latch mechanism

Cowl Area and Roof

A depressed area in the center of the hood allows air to enter the duct in the cowl section of the 911/912. On coupe models this air exits through vents above the rear window. Changes made for the 1969 model year were necessitated by improvements in the ventilation system which were not overtly apparent.

Windshield and cowl, 911 coupe

On the Targa model, the cowl and the windshield frame were separate stampings, while on coupe models they were made with the top as a single unit. The optional sunroof top utilized its own stamping and was not installed by an outside subcontractor as was the case with the 356 models.

Sunroof

The earliest 911s and 912s could be ordered with an optional sliding steel sunroof. This electrically operated unit came complete with an aluminum pop-up air deflector designed to reduce the air flow into the cockpit and control noise and buffeting.

Pop-up air deflector on 911 sunroof

On the earliest cars the rear drains exited through slits above the quarter windows similar to 356 models. This is not shown in the parts books and these drains were rerouted at some point after the 1967 models were introduced, so they no longer went through the exterior body panels but instead, emptied into the inner rear fender well.

Rear sunroof drain, early 911

There were no changes in components of the sunroof from 1965 to 1973. The only variation between cars were the fuzzy strips around the perimeter of the sunroof insert. Grey was used exclusively through 1968. From 1969 through 1973 black and grey were available such that the one most complementary to the exterior paint could be used.

Targa Top

When introduced in 1967, the Targa was a unique approach to open air driving. The folding top was designed to be easily removed and folded to fit within the luggage compartment. These first Targas featured a folding or "soft" rear window similar to those found in most convertibles. Were it not for the integral roll bar, it would have been a true cabriolet.

All tops were covered with black vinyl, which varied in composition and texture year to year. Only one change is noted in the parts book, and that is for the 1972 model year. The top itself had four changes on U.S. vehicles and three for the rest of the world. Porsche's chassis numbering system had become reasonably complicated by the time the first change was made at chassis numbers 11 850 160, 11 855 037, 11 860 143, 11 880 083, 112 870 438 and 11 870 134, all in mid-1968. The differences were improvements to the light metal folding frame and change of headliner material. Early headliners were black perforated vinyl while the later versions were a black foam-like material. No change was made in attachment points or hardware making it possible to interchange these tops.

Targa with soft window up

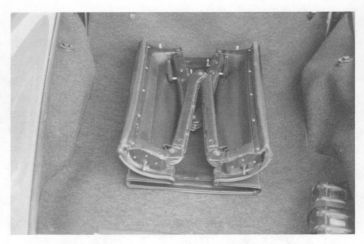

Folded, the Targa top stored within the luggage compartment. Note the perforated vinyl headliner

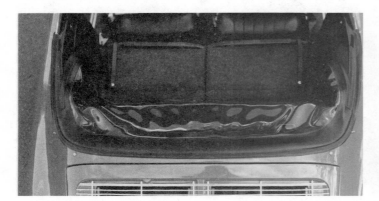

Folded soft window

Foam-like headliner material on later top

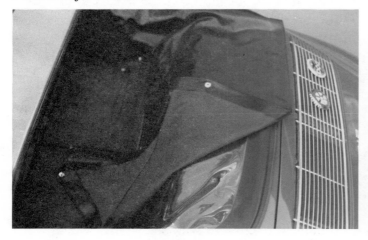

A vinyl boot covered the window when folded. It attached to the body with Tenax fasteners

The Targa top in place. Note leather-grain texture

The next change occurred in July 1969, an extensive redesign of frame, gutters and seals. All seals, including windshield frame seal, front roll bar seal and side window seals were new and improved. Except for the plastic escutcheon on the windshield frame, the mounting hardware was unchanged. The headliner and outer covering vinyl remained unaltered.

The final change in tops came in 1973, involving only the outer covering vinyl and two cover plates on the top's leading edge.

Doors, Rocker Panels

The doors on coupes and Targas were structurally identical, with only differing trim and hardware. From 1965 to 1973 there were only two different doors. A substantial number of trim and hardware changes occurred at the 1969 model year (see pages 67-69 for description of the interior trim). There was no significant alteration of the door structure or its size or shape.

The classic 911/912 profile. Doors and rocker panels made no significant changes

Rocker panels on all 911 and 912 models have a "C" shaped cross section and make up not only the outer sheet metal below the door, but also the outermost sill panel. While the line of the rocker panel continues from the front of the door to the leading edge of the rear wheel arch, the actual rocker panel stops just about where the back of the door starts upward. The rear part of the rocker panel is part of the rear quarter panel. This can be verified by looking forward into the rear wheel arch.

Lockposts

Left lockpost on 1965 911. Note recess and round lid release knob

LWB lockpost with depressed area and plastic T-handle

The lockpost or door jamb is the body panel behind the door on which the door latch mechanism mounts. The 1965-'68 parts book shows rear quarter panels both with and without lockposts, but not just lockposts. This hampers the restoration of this vintage car because the left side panel for early cars is not identical to that on 1969 and later cars. The difference involves

the circular depression where the rear lid pull lives. The early cars have a round recessed area, while the later cars have a flattened area. 1965 cars had a round release knob. This was changed to the familiar T-handle in 1966 and remained unaltered through 1973. Lockposts are not shown as a separate purchasable panel until the 1972-73 parts book. And then, oddly enough, the right lockpost, peculiar to the 1972 911 with a push release for the oil tank lid, is not listed.

Right side lockpost

The ill-fated 1972 lockpost with push-button release for oil filler

Coupe lockposts are listed, since they have the extension which goes to the top, but this is easily removed for installation on Targas. They are also easily retrofitted to pre-1972 cars since size and shape are identical. As mentioned above, on SWB cars, originality suffers if the driver's side lockpost is replaced.

Rear Quarter Panels

As stated in the section on lockposts, the 1965-68 parts books offered quarter panels with or without lockposts for coupes. The Targa quarter panels had slightly different contours where the rear window fits so an additional listing is present for these. The Targa quarter panels were available only with lockpost.

In 1969 the lengthening of the wheelbase caused a substantial modification to the rear quarter panel. The most obvious change was the repositioning of the rear wheel arches 57mm rearward. The flaring of the arch was also slightly wider to allow installation of wider rear wheels. The taillight box of the SWB car was replaced by a bracket similar to the front fender treatment of signal light mounting. The quarter panels remained unchanged through the 1973 model on the left side and through the 1971 model on the right side. These quarter panels came only with lockposts in place, except for

The SWB rear quarter panel

the right side Targa panel, which could be obtained with or without lockpost.

The LWB Targa rear cowl and quarter panel. Note different contours and slight flare

For 1972, Porsche moved the oil tank from behind the right rear wheel to in front of it. This made it necessary to install a filler door similar to the gas filler lid on the left front fender. The release knob was recessed in the right lockpost. This noble experiment has been acknowledged as a failure due to the propensity for service station attendants to put the wrong petroleum product in the oil tank. But for whatever the reason, for 1973, the oil tank was promptly moved back to its previous location. The quarter panel part numbers do not revert to the 1969-'71 numbers although no changes are apparent.

The 1972 911 featured a filler door for the oil tank

Different rear quarter panels were found on the Carrera 2.7 coupe and Targa built in 1973. These, of course, featured flared rear arches. The flares, referred to as "welding plates" in the parts book, are also offered as separate components.

In 1973 these flares looked big, the Carrera RS

One last part of the rear quarter panel is the steel cover which fills the torsion bar access hole. This was identical on all models except the Carrera, which had a "flared" cover.

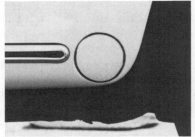

Torsion bar cover and seal

Rear Cowl, Rear Lid

The rear cowl area on the coupe is actually an extension of the roof panel below the rear window. On the Targa, however, an actual piece traverses the area above the rear lid and between the rear quarter panels. It is the same on all Targas 1967 through 1973 regardless of whether or not the rear window was "soft" or "fixed".

The rear lid for 911/912s built prior to mid-1968 is easily identified by the structural bar separating the two halves of the air intake under the grille. This area was painted satin-finish black on some 911s and 912s during the 1966 and 1967 model years. In 1967 and 1968 it was generally the same color as the lid. A different rear lid is listed for cars fitted with Sportomatic transmissions, likely due to holes for the extra script. An unmentioned change occurred in 1967 when all lids received a modification to the substructure to accommodate the optional rear wiper.

The bar was removed in the version fitted to mid-1968 through 1973 cars. This was fairly early in the 1968 production at chassis numbers 11 800 379, 11 805 122, 11 810 290, 11 820 368, 11 830 260, 11

The rubber seal mounted on the rear lid was deleted early in production

Inner structure of the 1965-66 style rear lid

This bracket was added to mount the rear wiper for the 1967 model year

Satin black painted area under rear grille, 1967 912

850 118, 11 855 030, 11 860 107, 11 870 093, 11 880 064, 12 820 159, 12 870 337 and 12 801 832. From 1969 through 1971 only the 912, 911T and 911E had steel rear lids, while the costlier 911S had one fashioned from aluminum. A steel lid was used on the 1972 and 1973 911S. The 1971 911T and 911E used the same lid as the earlier 911T, but the 1972 and 1973 models had a different part number although there is no apparent difference in the outer skin or inner structure.

Inner structure of the "barless" rear lid. Pneumatic strut can be seen on left side hinge

Air conditioning brought with it new work for the pneumatic strut on the rear lid. The heavy condensor inspired many owners to install tandem struts

One final lid was the "ducktail" spoiler fitted to the 1973 Carrera model. It was made of fiberglass reinforced plastic.

Hinges are similar to those found on the front hood, although only one, the left side, has a pneumatic strut. The latch mechanism is also similar to the one used on the front hood although there was no safety latch device. It does incorporate that clever mechanism that automatically releases if the cable breaks. Hinges and latch mechanism did not change between 1965 and 1973.

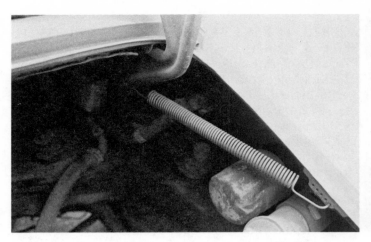

This 901 prototype used a spring instead of the pneumatic strut to hold the rear lid up

The 1973 Carrera RS featured this controversial looking rear lid

Rear latch mechanism

Inner structure of the "ducktail" spoiler

INNER BODY AND CHASSIS

Inner Nose and Luggage Compartment

Inner nose panel, 1965 912

The 911/912 carried on the tradition of unit-body construction started by the 356. With the exception of the front fenders, lids and doors, the external body panels are actually part of the chassis of the car. To make things a little easier to comprehend, we'll separate outer and inner body panels rather than body and chassis.

Up front, one encounters the inner nose panel, in which the lower front hood latch is mounted. The bracket that holds the center section of the front bumper to body seal is welded to the front of this panel. The only change that was made to this part was the appearance of a round opening on the left side through which the neck of the windshield washer reservoir extended. This change occurred at the beginning of the 1968 model year.

Making up the bottom of of the front chassis section is the forward part of the floor pan stamping. Generally referred to as the "front suspension pan", this name has become synonymous for "extensive (and often expensive) rust repair." This area is a critical part of the

unit body since the entire front suspension and steering bolt directly to it. The depressed "U" shaped channel that separates the front mounting locations for the left and right A-frames serves as an area for condensation and subsequently rust. The gas tank support above the pan is also involved in the problem.

There are a number of different floor pans listed from 1965 through 1973, including different versions for left and right hand steering, differences between 911 and 912 and year differences. Actual variations are subtle, usually consisting of changes in brackets, pedal location etc. Length and width were unaltered. A towing hook was located in the center between the front A-frame mounts.

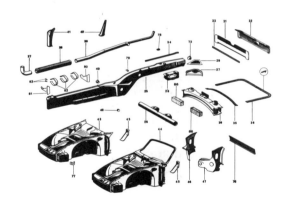

Illustration 8/1, 1965-68 Parts Book

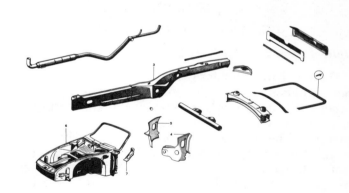

Illustration 8/1, 1969 Parts Book

Illustration 8/1, 1965-68 Parts Book

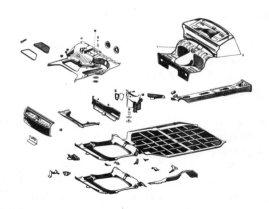

Illustration 8/1, 1969 Parts Book

Front suspension area. Note towing hook and rubber drains. Drains were forward of the U-channel

The fuel tank support on 1965 through 1968 911/912 models differed from later versions by having a small bracket to locate and secure the battery on the left side. 911 and 912 models had different supports.

Battery bracket, 1967 911S

The inner front fender located the front shock absorber and also acted as the upper suspension pivot. Its other main functions are to be an integral part of the stressed chassis and to locate front fenders and front bumper. The first cars did not have an adjustment provision for the top shock absorber mount. This situation was rectified mid-1965 at chassis numbers 302 694, 351 292 and 451 373. On 1965 through 1968 cars a bracket was welded to the inner fender on which to bolt the bumper. The fender bolts to the top of the inner fender and to a vertical fender joining panel welded to the back.

Targa models had a steel reinforcing bar bolted under the dashboard to help stabilize the open car's chassis. The difference between coupe and Targa models in the inner fender panel is for the mounting point of this bar.

The inner fender was substantially changed in 1969 when tandem batteries moved in, one on each side. Differences are noted for Targa models, as explained above, and for right sides on right-hand drive cars. Because of the placement of the batteries, the bumper mounting hardware was changed substantially. A change was noted between the 1969 and 1970 models, but no changes occurred from then until 1973.

The LWB battery, hiding behind the wiring

Attached to the rear of the of the inner fender is the hinge post on which the doors mount. Coupes and Targas have the same part. A change is noted for the left side in 1969 and the right side in 1970.

Hinge post, 1965 911

The rear floor of the luggage compartment had a number of changes in early production. Left hand drive cars were changed at chassis number 308 070 and 500 419, a mid-1967 change. Another change occurred at the introduction of the 1968 models. In 1969 the all new forced air ventilation system brought additional changes. A final change was made at the introduction of the 1973 model year.

Right hand drive (RHD) cars were quite different for obvious reasons. Rather than a mirror image panel, however, a substantially different part was constructed. There was no large door which covered a gasoline heater, but instead a small lid that housed only the master cylinder reservoir. There was only a single change in the RHD panel, and that corresponded to the 1969 change which involved ventilation system as in LHD cars.

Luggage compartment, 1965 912

Luggage compartment, 1966 911 with gasoline heater

Luggage compartment 1969-73

Driver's Compartment

The floor pan was mentioned in the discussion on the front suspension pan. There was no significant change in this part during this time span, and the same floor was used in coupe and Targa models. Thickness was approximately 20-gauge, as is the majority of sheet metal comprising both body and chassis.

The central tunnel not only acts to give rigidity to the chassis but also locates seat rails, hand brake and shift mechanism while serving as a conduit for wiring, cables and hydraulic and fuel lines. Changes are subtle in this area. Right and left hand drive are once again different and starting in 1969, U.S. specification cars are different from the non-U.S. cars. Again there was no significant change in dimensions or shape, but rather those variations that occurred were due to equipment

fitted.

Because the roof was not involved as a part of the unit body, Targas had some additional strengthening panels. Up front they were in the driver's and passenger's footwell area, as shown in illustration 8/1 of the factory parts book (page 13). Because of their presence, the width dimension of this area is smaller than the coupe by about four inches. Another pair of strengthening panels are in the inner rear quarter panel area alongside the rear jump seats. These are seen in illustration 8/2T of the parts book.

8/2 T   GRUPPE · GROUP · GROUPE · GRUPPO **8**

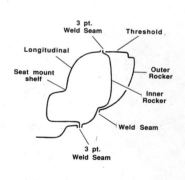

Illustration 8/2T, 1969 Parts Book

Making up the outer sides of the passenger compartment was a box section made of the following components (inside to outside): longitudinal member, inner rocker panel and outer rocker panel. Between the longitudinal member and the inner rocker was the tube that supplied heated air to the passenger's compartment. About an inch of the inner rocker panel is visible below the outer rocker panel where it welds to the floor pan. Like the outer rocker panel described on page 9, the inner rocker panel was identical on all years and models.

Longitudinal cross section

The longitudinal member is another story. Numerous changes were made in this part due to revisions in heater system, powertrain and suspension. The part runs from the front of the passenger compartment to the rear of the engine compartment. Among its functions are: location of the outer seat rails, making up the inner sill panel, location of heat outlets on SWB cars, location for the housing containing the rear torsion bars and support of the engine. Because of its many talents, numerous changes occurred. To list all variations would serve little function, since to the restorer, in all likelihood, the necessity to replace this part would tend to make one question the candidate's potential.

A major change took place in 1969 when the heater system and rear suspension were both substantially modified. The pipe which carries warm air also made a substantial change as can be seen by the illustrations in the parts book. 911s differed from 912s due to the position of rear motor mounts, which in the latter were located farther forward. Targas and coupes also differed in this area due to the altered rear inner structure.

The rear seat area and deck area doubled as a firewall. Targas differed from coupes, and cars fitted with Sportomatic transmissions had a different stamping than those with manual gearboxes. An alteration was made at the SWB/LWB change. Unfortunately, this chassis section disappeared from the parts manuals about that time, so subsequent alterations cannot be noted.

The brushed stainless steel Targa band covers an actual roll bar which is an integral part of the chassis. A change took place in mid-year 1968 at chassis numbers 11 850 065, 11 870 040, 11 855 016 and 12 870 207. The only additional change was in 1969 when the outer covering added vents. There were different roll bars for fixed and soft windows due to the very different mounting for the two window types. The two alternate bars are listed from 1969 through 1971 with the fixed window type only in 1972 and 1973.

Targa bar SWB   *Targa bar LWB*

Rear Chassis

The rear torsion bars were housed in a cylinder which doubled as the inner pivot point for the rear control arms (bananas) of the rear suspension. The tor-sion bar tube was altered for the 1969 model when wheelbase changed, and again for the 1973 model, although no corresponding change was made to either control arms or torsion bars on the latter.

Rear shocks attached to a box-section bulkhead that is visible in front of the engine. This part was the same for coupe and Targa, right and left hand drive, with changes in 1969 and 1970.

Engine mounts were in the rear corners of the engine compartment of 911s. They consist of a corner bracket which holds a flexible mount. There was no change made between 1965 and 1973.

911 engine mount

The engine mounts on 912 models were farther forward, due to the shorter engine, and consisted of a bracket welded to the longitudinal member. Originally, the bracket held the same flexible mount that held the 911 engine with a pressed steel bracket bolted directly to the crankcase of the engine. At engine numbers 746 700 and 832 814 (April 1966) this was modified; the outer mounts were then rigid with four flexible blocks between the engine and redesigned mounting bracket. There was no change to the bracket on the longitudinal since the rigid mounting bracket bolted directly to the same holes that the flexible mounts did.

Early 912 engine mount

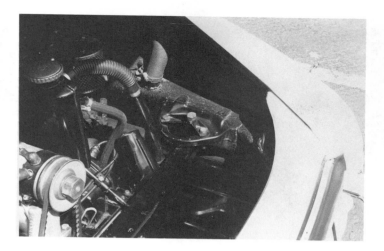

Late 912 engine mount

Bracket for mounting 912 engine (late)

The rear latch panel, which holds the lower rear lid latch and those wonderful gold foil decals (which appeared in 1967), was unaltered from 1965 through 1973. The earliest cars did not feature the six depressions where the decals would subsequently be located. This change is not acknowledged by the parts book, but occurred early in the 1965 model year. It and the upper portion of the front inner nose panel are the only chassis components that are painted body color and not covered with black PVC.

Rear latch panel with no impressions, # 300 149

The last chassis component that we will describe is the rear inner fender or quarter panel. As alluded to in the section on the driver's compartment, Targa models had an extra strengthening panel on each side. A change in this strengthening panel occurred at the 1972 model year, according to the parts books, but it is not obvious what it was. The quarter panel was also sub-

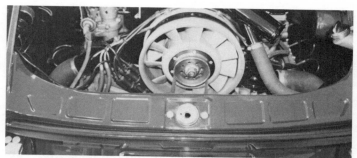

Rear latch panel, 1965 911, impressions, no decals

stantially different because of the roll bar attachment and differences in rear window treatment.

911 and 912 models were substantially different due to the dry sump, electronic ignition and electric fuel pump on the 911. The sump and oil filter was in the right rear quarter and the electrical components on the left.

Left side inner fender replete with electronics and fuel system components. Also, foil decals

911 oil filler and filter, 1965

911 oil tank, right rear inner fender, 1966

Changes in the 911 coupe inner rear quarter occurred at chassis number 305 796, 1969 model, 1970 model (left side only), 1972 (right side due to oil tank), 1973 (right side due to oil tank). The Carrera and 911S of 1973 shared a different right side inner quarter due to modifications necessary for the oil lines for the front mounted oil cooler. Targa changes mirrored those found in coupes except for the 1970 left side change.

EXTERIOR TRIM

Front Bumper

Front bumpers on the earliest 911 and 912 models had an ornamental strip made from bright anodized aluminum and vinyl. It was identical in cross section to the trim strip used on 356B and C models. Two versions were listed in the 1965-68 parts book, one with holes for bumper guard mounting bolts and one without. A third, much wider, variety was introduced in 1967 on the 911S. In 1968 911S models were not imported to the U.S. due to those nice folks at the E.P.A. The wider trim strip was used on the European 911S and optional on the U.S. and European 911L. This, in conjunction with a number of other trim pieces that will be described as we go from front to back, were collectively referred to as "S-trim". This molding was described in the 1969-71 parts books as standard equipment on the 911E and 911S and not optional on the 911T or 912; however, it was undoubtedly fitted to these models, as well. In 1972 this trim was standard only on the 911S but was optional on both the 911E and 911T. In 1973 it was again optional on the 911T and 911E and was standard on 911S and Carrera 2.7 models. U.S. cars with this trim had the area under the bumper guards cut out on 1973 models due to the enlarged rubber bumper guards necessitated by bumper regulations provided by those other nice folks at the D.O.T.

1972 911 with S-trim

Plain chrome bumper guard standard on U.S.-spec 911 and 912 models

1965 911 with standard bumper trim and no guards

In countries other than the U.S., front bumper guards were optional. In the 1965-68 parts book two types of front guards are listed. The first, all-chrome, version was standard on all U.S. cars in 1966, the year when the 911/912 was introduced in America. All other countries had this guard optional from 1965 through 1968. In 1967, the other guard, chrome with a rubber cover, became standard on 911 and 912 models in the U.S.; a similar version became optional elsewhere. A fourth variety was the guard for "S-trim". These were all of the rubber covered variety and differed only in the cut-out for the trim strip.

Late style rubber-covered bumper guard with cut out for S-trim

By 1969 the U.S. version guards described above became optional for the rest of the world. The all-chrome guards are listed as standard equipment for 912, 912 U.S. and 911T. The chrome guard with rubber pad was listed as optional for these models. The 911E and 911S have the guard described above for use with "S-trim". This scenario covered the years 1969 to 1971. All guards had a black plastic panel on the rear of the upper part.

For non-U.S. cars there were four types of optional

18

Early style all-metal guard. Note vent at top

1967 911 with plastic backed bumper guard. Chrome tube is an aftermarket accessory

on plastic receptacles inserted into the top of the housing. There were three versions of this light unit. The U.S. version lens was amber, while the one used for Italy was totally clear. The rest of the world got one that had a clear parking light on the inside of the lens and amber turnsignal on the outside. All featured a white sponge-rubber seal that separated the light unit from the front fender.

SWB U.S. turn signal unit

guards during the 1972 and 1973 model years. These were different from the previous version. The 911S and Carrera 2.7 could be equipped with guards designed for use with "S-trim" in either chrome or black, with rubber pads. 911T and 911E models could have either of these or if fitted with standard bumper trim, black and chrome versions were also available. On 1973 U.S. specification cars, a synthetic foam rubber bumper guard replaced the metal ones on earlier Porsches. Two versions were made; one for standard trim and one for S-trim. They were a stop gap measure for D.O.T. crash protection mandates and were destined to be used for only a single year.

In 1969 the change in front fenders also included a change in turn signal units. These were considerably different in construction, though similar in appearance. Also manufactured by Bosch, these units had a removable lens, which made replacement due to breakage or fading considerably less costly. Bulbs were mounted in the back alloy housing. Bulb replacement required removal of the lens rather than the entire unit as in earlier cars. The seal on these units was black rubber. The chrome rim around the lens was not metal, as in the earlier light, but was vacuum-metalized onto the outer edge of the plastic lens. In 1973 this chrome trim was replaced by black on all models. The three varieties of lenses which were described above prevailed.

Optional black chrome bumper guard (rear)

Rubber 1973 front bumper guard

All front bumper guards were sided due to the curvature of the bumper. They mount to the bumper with two bolts each.

LWB turn signal with chrome trim was used 1969-72

Front Turn signals and Horn Grilles

The first 911s and 912s had a turn signal unit produced by Bosch. The plastic lens was melted to the housing and was not removable. Bulbs were mounted

Black trimmed 1973 European-spec. turn signal

Early four screw horn grille. U.S.-spec. glass covered headlight unit

SWB two screw horn grille. Early Bosch assymetric headlight

To the inside of the turn signal unit was a grille behind which the horn could be found. Porsche could trace this tradition back to 1954 when grilles first appeared on the 356. On the first 911s and 912s they were chrome-plated brass and were secured to the front fender by four phillips-head screws, one in each corner. These were used in 1965 and 1966. A change to a less expensive pot metal casting, which was mounted by two phillips-head screws, occurred some time mid-1966 (first car on our owner survey with 2 screw grilles is 303468). The exact time that this occurred is not noted by the parts book nor is the corresponding change to the front fender, which required brackets to mount the grilles. A special version of this style grille was installed for cars that had upper mounted fog or driving lights. These had the center section of the middle bars removed where the lights were mounted. A grey sponge-rubber seal was fitted between the top edge of the grille and the fender on two screw mounted grilles. Four screw mounted grilles had two small black rubber buffers on the inside mounting points.

The 1969 revision of fender and turnsignal brought with it a change in horn grille. The new grille was similar to the previous version in appearance and construction but was narrower by nearly an inch because the signal unit had grown by the same amount. Like the previous grille, there was a version designed to ac-

commodate upper mounted fog and driving lights. A similar but shorter rubber profile was used between grille and fender.

By 1972 the grilles had become vacuum-metal plated plastic, then in 1973 they became black plastic. The grille listed for cars with fog or driving lights bore the same part number as the earlier metal version, and no black version was mentioned. The same rubber profile was used on the plastic version grille as was used on the 1969 through 1971 metal grille.

Headlights

A variety of headlight units were used on the 900 series Porsche. When initially introduced, four different units were used. The majority of the world got a Bosch asymmetric unit, and the RHD countries received one designed for left-hand traffic. French specification cars utilized yellow bulbs. A Hella sealed beam unit similar to the one found on 356s and Volkswagens (with a slightly wider rim), was used on U.S. specification cars due to the D.O.T.s insistence that sealed beam headlights were best. For the rest of the world a non-sealed beam headlight replacement could be inserted into this Hella unit, implying that one could specify this type unit as an option.

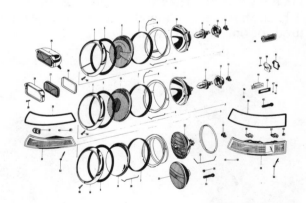

Illustration 9/6, 1965-68 Parts Book

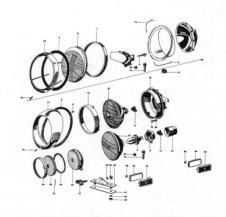

Illustration 9/6, 1965-68 Parts Book

LWB chrome horn grille. Post-67 sealed beam headlight unit with wide chrome rim

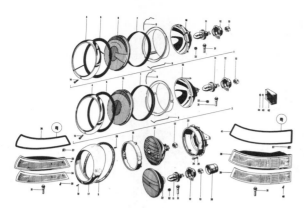

Illustration 9/6, 1972-73 Parts Book

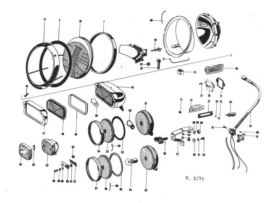

Illustration 9/6, 1972-73 Parts Book

For the 1968 model year there was a new headlight unit produced by Bosch for the 911S. This is commonly referred to as an H-1 unit due to its use of two H-1 type halogen bulbs which function independently for high and low beams. Three varieties of this light unit were offered; one for countries with right-hand traffic, one for countries with left-hand traffic and one with a yellow lens for France, which apparently has a D.O.T. of its own. Speaking of such, in 1968 it became unlawful in the U.S. for the coveted sealed beam to be covered by glass because the glass might distort and further weaken the obsolete light unit's output. In response, Porsche introduced its first ever uncovered sealed beam. The wide chrome rim and adjuster were again made by Hella. Again, a non-sealed beam replacement unit was listed as optional.

LWB car with H-1 headlight unit. Note Hella fog light mounted in horn grille

For 1969 the 912 was the only Porsche to continue to use the non-halogen Bosch asymmetrical units described earlier. U.S. versions shared the same sealed beam arrangement as did the 1968 model and indeed all subsequent U.S. specification cars through 1973. For the rest of the world, all 911 models received the H-1 unit used on the 1968 911S.

In 1970 the H-1 unit was modified. There were again three configurations; one for right-hand traffic, one for left-hand traffic and one with a yellow lens for France. These continued as standard equipment on all models up to 1973 for non-U.S. markets. The non-sealed beam replacement for sealed beam light units was dropped in 1971, although a left hand traffic sealed beam was added. In 1972 and 1973 an optional, more powerful 60/50-watt sealed beam unit for right-hand traffic was added to the standard 50/40-watt unit. The parts book does not specify that these were not intended for use on the U.S. specification cars. It also does not seemed to be linked to a specific model, implying that they could be requested on any model.

In 1973 the H-4 headlight unit was fitted as standard equipment for all countries except France and the U.S. It was differentiated from the now optional H-1 in a number of ways. The fundamental difference was the use of a single H-4 halogen bulb. Outwardly, the H-4 unit could be identified by its lens and by the two adjustment screws on the rim. The H-1 had four. Early H-4 units did not have the pebble grain texture at the top of the lens of subsequent years.

The 1973 H-4 headlight unit

Fog Lights

In 1965, fog lights were standard equipment on all 911s, located in the lower front bumper area. They were the familiar Hella 128 light unit used on 356B and C models. There were four varieties, all using the same fluted clear lens and chrome outer housing. The difference was in the bulb and reflector. U.S. cars had a "white" reflector and tungsten bulb. The standard configuration for Europe was a similar unit with a yellow reflector. It is not inherently obvious why U.S. cars could not be so fitted, since yellow fog lights were not illegal. Two other varieties not available for the U.S. market were the more powerful halogen units with an H-3 bulb, available with either white or yellow reflectors.

21

The Hella 128 fog light

SWB grille-mounted fog light *SWB grille-mounted driving light*

Three other light units, installed in the horn grille areas, were available for non-U.S. specification cars. Two fog light units, one with white and one with yellow reflectors, were offered. Both utilized H-3 halogen bulbs as did a driving light version which was also available.

In 1969 the Hella 128s were replaced by Hella 169 units, which were similar in appearance. The differences were in their larger size and change in mounting location. 128s were mounted from the top of the unit, while 169s mounted from the rear. According to the parts books, two varieties of 169s were available. Both used halogen bulbs and are listed as being not available for the U.S. or Holland. Like the earlier 128

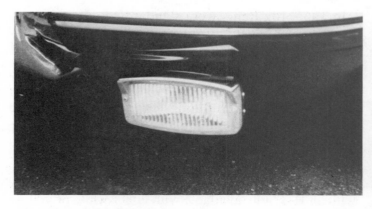

The Hella 169 fog light

unit, a white or yellow reflector was available. All had fluted clear lenses. This light remained optional through 1973, although it could not be fitted with the 911S type spoiler bumper in 1972 and 1973, since no "holes" were present.

The round fog lights mounted in the horn grille area in 1969 were identical to those used in previous years. A round fog light was also added with a removable tungsten bulb for the U.S. market. In 1970 these changed, at least in part number. No change in lens, bulb or housing is noted. In 1971 though, a bulb change was made in the U.S. unit. No further alterations occurred.

Modification to the horn grille when fogs present

Round fog lights and driving lights for the rest of the world had halogen bulbs. As previously stated, the 1969 version was identical to the earlier versions. In 1970 a number of changes took place. The majority of countries got an H-3 powered unit with a clear lens in either fog or driving conformation. For French Porschephiles there were identical units with yellow lenses. The final permutation was for Italian specification cars. These light units featured 55w H-1 bulbs. No additional changes were made through 1973.

Hood Crest

The Porsche crest that adorned the front hood of the 1965-1973 911/912 was a larger version of the one found on the 356 model. It was secured by two press-on fasteners and had a vinyl seal between it and the painted surface. There were no modifications between 1965 and 1973. It is, perhaps, worth mentioning that the color of the red bars was a red-orange color rather than the deep red found on later and reproduction hood crests.

Original hood crest *Reproduction hood crest*

Cowl Area

The cowl area carries three trim items, the fresh air vent, the windshield washer nozzles and the wiper arms. The first item, the fresh air vent, consisted of an outer frame and a screen. The parts books state that these did not change from 1965 through 1973. This is fundamentally true but not one hundred percent accurate. When first introduced, both frame and screen were a dull anodized aluminum finish. Apparently, these were painted black in 1966 and 1967 and are commonly are found with flaking paint. To remedy this later models had anodized black versions. This change is not documented. Other than that, no changes occurred.

The washer nozzles used were carried over from the 356C. They were made from black rubber and had an anodized aluminum dome. Twin jets directed the water spray, and a check valve mounted below the cowl kept water from draining back to the reservoir. (Reservoirs are described on page 41) There were two washers on each car, mounted to the outside of the wiper shafts. No changes were made from 1965 through 1973.

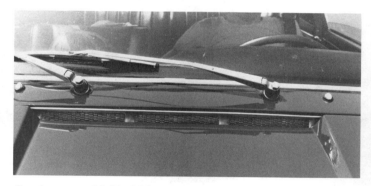

Cowl area, 1967 911

The front wiper system on 1965-67 911/912 models consisted of a motor and crank assembly. The arms were painted silver, as was the metal portion of the blades. Blades were available from both Bosch and SWF. The wipers had three speeds with no interval function available. Right and left-hand drive cars had different motors and crank mechanisms although they used the same arms and both parked on the right side.

For the 1968 model year silver was replaced by black for wiper arms, blades and the cap nut that held on the wiper arm. Also at this time, there was a difference between LHD and RHD cars; the wipers now parked on the side of the car in which the driver sat. Arms and blades were supplied by both Bosch and SWF. It is also worth noting that the left wiper arm for LHD cars was the same as the right for RHD. This arm was straight while the inside arm was bent at the wiper end so that it would be more parallel to the cowl when parked. There was no change to the motor or crank assembly.

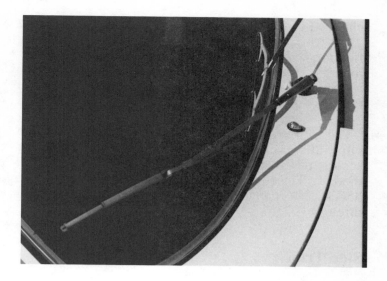

Right parking silver wipers, 1967 912

In 1969 the motor and crank assembly changed, but the wiper arms and blades remained the same. The same items changed again in 1970. 1971 brought a step backward to the 1969 motor and yet another crank mechanism. Both arms and blades changed, and only SWF remained as manufacturer. The change in arms and blades was to the part numbers assigned to the 914 model. The earlier arm/blade units can all be interchanged since the mount area never changed. No further changes were made through 1973.

Left parking black wipers, 1972 911

Windshield

The windshield on the 911/912 was identical on both coupe and Targa models. Very few modifications were made in this area. The standard windshield was clear glass; as an option, a tinted version was available. The tinted windshield was pale green all over with no darker sun screen band at the top. These two windshield types were unchanged from 1965 through 1973. In 1971 only, an optional heated windshield was listed.

The rubber seal surrounding the windshield was

changed for the U.S. and Puerto Rico in 1969. Since glass, trim and body were not changed, the only modification was to the inner lip of the seal, which was longer. This was to accommodate the D.O.T., which asserted that the windshield should stay on the car in the event of a frontal assault.

The trim was made up of two outer halves and two clips; all were bright anodized aluminum. The cross section of the trim was identical to that used on 356C models. The clips were actually the same ones used on 356Cs. No changes were made in this area from 1965 through 1973.

Side Trim

The items covered in this section will be wheel arch and rocker panel moldings, scripts, stripes, outside mirrors, side reflectors and door handles. Side windows will be covered next.

Wheel arch moldings were first offered as optional equipment on the 1969 911E and 911S. They were made of bright anodized aluminum and mounted with aluminum pop-rivets. They were available as options on 1970 and 1971 911E and 911S and all 1972 and 1973 models except the Carrera 2.7.

Optional wheel arch molding

The rocker panel moldings used on all 1965 through 1967 911/912 models were similar to the ones on 356B/Cs. They consisted of a bright anodized aluminum housing with a vinyl insert and a vinyl base seal. They were mounted to the rocker panel with sheet metal screws and located with the leading edge just barely ahead of the junction between the front fender and the rocker panel. Their trailing edges stopped ahead of the rear torsion bar access cover. These were also standard equipment on the 1968 912, 911 and 911T; 1969-'71 912 and 911T and 1972-'73 911T and 911E.

1967 911S models had a rocker panel trim with a wider rubber insert and different base than the standard molding. It was similar in length and was unique to

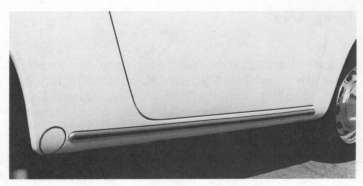

Standard rocker panel molding, 1967 912

Rocker panel molding, 1967 911S

S-trim rocker panel moldings, 1968-73

that year and model. By early 1968, the "S-trim" rocker panel molding was an anodized aluminum extrusion which covered the entire rocker panel. It featured a wide rubber insert mounted close to the top. Between the top edge and the body was a vinyl extrusion identical to the one used on bumper moldings. Aluminum caps, which were mounted by sheet metal screws, held these in place at leading and trailing ends. It again was used on only the 911S or, in the U.S., the 911L models (optional).

By 1969, the wide aluminum S-trim was used on both 911E and 911S models. It was necessary to lengthen the moldings due to the extended wheelbase. There was no other change, and the end caps were identical to those used in 1968. As with the bumper moldings, from 1969 through 1971, S-trim rocker panel moldings were standard on 911E and 911S cars. In 1972 and 1973 they were standard on 911S and optional on 911T and 911E. The Carrera 2.7 featured

"Bent" Carrera side molding

Carrera "negative" stripe

similar moldings which were "bent" at the trailing ends to accommodate the mild flares.

The only scripts found on the sides of the 911/912 models were on Targa models. When they first appeared on the sides of the roll bar in 1967, they were gold anodized aluminum. The lone change was at the 1972 model year, when gold was replaced by black anodized aluminum.

Black Targa script

It is uncertain when the use of side stripes first appeared. Both black and white "positive" stripes were offered in all parts manuals from 1967 through 1973. Their appearance seems to be linked to the introduction of the 911R in 1967. They are referred to as "positive" to contrast them with the "negative" stripes used on later cars. The positive stripes feature the extended Porsche lettering in either black or white with a solid stripe above and below. In the negative stripe, which appeared in 1974, the Porsche lettering was silhouetted by the die-cut stripe making the letters body color. In

Positive stripes first appeared on this car, the 911R

addition, in 1973 the Carrera 2.7 featured a "Carrera" negative side stripe that was in the same script as the nameplate on the rear lid. They were offered in blue, red or green (to match the wheel centers) and only applied to Carreras painted Grand Prix White. In all cases these stripes were optional. Carreras could be fitted with "Porsche" positive stripes if so desired.

The optional outside rear-view mirror was mounted on the driver's door. The standard mirror used from 1965 through 1967 was the same Durant mirror used on the 356C. From 1968 through 1971, a slightly larger Durant mirror, also round, was fitted. The base was identical, and the seal between the mirror and the body was the same as the earlier version. In 1971, it could be fitted with a convex mirror.

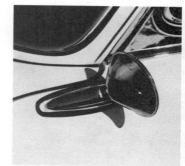

Early Durant mirror

Late Durant mirror

Optional Talbot mirror

Rectangular side mirror used in 1972-73

A Talbot mirror was offered from 1965 through 1968. Both right and left mirrors are listed in the accessories catalogs, along with text stating that they were not installed at the factory, but for $13.40 (1965 price) they were a bargain. In 1968 the left side Talbot mirror is noted as being illegal in the U.S. and Germany, due to its small glass size.

For 1972 and 1973, a rectangular mirror was fitted on the driver's door. It, like the Durant, had a brushed metal finish. The 1968-71 Durant mirror is also illustrated in the 1972 parts manual. It was available with either flat or convex mirror. From the description in the parts manual it is unclear if it was fitted only in Sweden or if it could be obtained as optional equipment in other venues.

Side reflectors were fitted on 1968 U.S.-specification 911 and 912 models. The front ones were amber, and the rear were red. They were added in response to D.O.T. regulations and were very much a last minute add-on. By 1969 the reflectors were incorporated into the turnsignal and taillight units.

Tacked on reflectors for 1968 U.S. cars only

1968 911L showing amber front and red rear reflectors. Note 911Ls did not come standard with S-trim

Door handles on the early 911 and 912 models were chrome-plated die cast zinc. Separate door handles were manufactured for those cars fitted with or without steering column locks (the same key was used for door and ignition). For 1965 and 1966 the area where the key was inserted was concave, while in 1967 it was convex. In 1968 our friends at D.O.T. legislated away push-button door handles in an effort to keep doors from opening in accidents. Due to this, a reasonably bulky door handle replaced the original design. It had two "wings" which left the push-button in a hole. Two varieties were made, one for cars with steering column lock and one for cars without. The final permutation was the trigger release handle of the 1970-73 911. It was chrome-plated zinc, as were the previous handles. The left and right door handles were different but

Early production door handle, subtly different from later cars

Later production door handle was bulkier than one on left

Winged door handle was used in 1968-69

Trigger type door handles appeared in the 1970 model year

shared the same left and right lock cylinders as the handles used in 1970 and 1971. The 1972 and 1973 handle was virtually identical in appearance, but the handles were now interchangeable right to left, and the lock cylinders were sided. Since all cars got steering column locks in 1970, there was no longer any duplication caused by this difference.

Side Windows and Associated Hardware

Prior to the 1969 model year, there were eight different varieties of the frame that mounted on the door that contained the vent window on coupes. Four have clear vent window glass and four have green tinted glass. The other changes are as follows: The first two varieties had frames of chrome-plated brass. The first type, described as "with wedge" was used until chassis # 302 805 for 911 and 351 271 for Porsche-bodied 912. This corresponds to a mid-1965 change. From that point until the 1968 model change version "without wedge" was used. The wedge was an extension inward, or flaring, at the rear of the window frame (see photos on next page).

For the 1968 model year, brass was replaced by bright anodized aluminum as the material of choice for window frames. A final change was made on U.S.-destined cars at chassis numbers 118 30 004, 128 20

26

Wedge   *No wedge*

Movable vent window, 1967 912   *Rubber covered handle, aluminum frame, 1968*

031, 118 05 001 and 128 00 240. The change consisted of putting a rubber-covered knob on the vent window catch. The timing was barely into the 1968 model year and was no doubt a result of our friends at the D.O.T. again. Only U.S.-specification cars received this covered knob.

The improved ventilation system of the 1969 model or, perhaps, just the lower cost to produce, prompted Porsche to abandon the movable vent window on coupes. This was the final change on coupe models. Like the 1968 versions, it was bright anodized aluminum.

Non-moving coupe vent window, 1969-73

Targas had the same variety of green tinted and non-tinted window combinations that coupes did through 1968. In 1969 tinted glass became standard. The only major change was for the 1969 model year. Like coupes, starting in 1968 U.S. models got rubber vent knob covers while the rest of the world suffered. Un-

like coupes, movable vent windows did not fall from favor in 1969 and continued to be used through 1973. The material was chrome plated brass on all years.

On coupes, a rubber and velvet channel, similar to the one used on 356 models, was fitted into the window frame, surrounding the side window on three sides. The rear and upper piece were modified for the 1968 model and all changed at the 1969 model year. It is important to note that all of these were a cloth and rubber combination and not the flocked rubber style used on later model cars. The changes for Targas mirrored those of the coupes. The channels on Targas made up only the front and lower rear (below the top of the door's sheet metal).

Side windows were available clear or tinted like all other glass. The only changes occurred at the 1968 model year in coupes and there were no changes at all on Targa models. An interesting option on Carrera 2.7 coupes was thinner 4.2-mm side glass.

Below the side window on both coupe and Targa is a molding which holds the side window squeegee. This part was chrome plated brass, and the squeegee was vinyl. A change to aluminum was made for the 1968 model year. There was also a difference between coupe and Targa models. In 1970 there was a change in the squeegee from vinyl to a rubber seal with a completely different cross section, although there was no corresponding change in the molding which held it.

Chrome door top with shrinking vinyl squeegee

Hinging rear quarter window

The hinging rear quarter windows used on coupe models were modified only one time between 1965 and 1973. At the 1968 model change the window frame was changed from chrome-plated brass to bright anodized aluminum. There was no change in mounting hardware or size and shape. As with the other windows, green tint or clear was available. The trim piece mounted below the window was also modified for the 1968 model year. Commemorative decals were mounted to the inner surface of the right rear quarter window on some 1971 and 1972 cars which declared Porsche World Champion for 1969 through 1970 (through 1971 on 1972 models). On Targas, these were mounted on the right side of the rear window alongside the roll bar.

World Champion decal, 1972

Quarter window latch, open

Quarter window latch, closed

Rear Window

The rear window of coupe models was nearly flat. As with all other windows, optional green tint was available. In 1967 a rear window with heat elements

was offered as optional equipment. The heat elements of this window were in vertical array. By the 1969 model year a 100-watt "single stage" window was fitted as standard equipment with a "two stage" (two heat settings) 100/250-watt unit optional. The latter was available only with tinted glass. The heat elements in these windows were horizontal in orientation. This scenario remained the same until 1973 on coupes. On the Carrera, an optional single stage 100-watt window with lightweight 4.2-mm thick glass was available.

Rear window, 911 coupe, note defogger wires

The seal and trim was similar to the front windshield. The only change noted is for the seal at the 1969 model year. It corresponds to the accommodation for the new wiring used for the heated rear window. The aluminum trim was identical in cross section to the front trim. The clips which cover the joint between left and right halves are the same as the front. The Carrera with thinner glass had seal and trim designed to fit only that model.

When the Targa model was introduced in 1967, it featured a fold-down vinyl rear window, making it nearly a true convertible. When folded, a vinyl boot covered the window. According to the parts manuals, this remained optional until 1971, although I am unaware of U.S. versions built later than the 1969 model year. The fixed (glass) window is illustrated in the 1965-68 parts book on a page dated 11/67. It is listed as being green tint with defogger. Like its coupe counterpart, the defogger wires were oriented in a vertical pattern. By 1969, a 100/250-watt two-stage rear defogger became an option. This replaced the 100-watt single stage unit as standard equipment in 1971.

The glass window was surrounded by a rubber seal. The bottom of the seal had a bright anodized aluminum molding of the same cross section used on the windshield trim. Running along the back of the roll bar was a seal which contacted the glass of the rear window. On "soft window" models this seal was considerably wider.

Soft window up

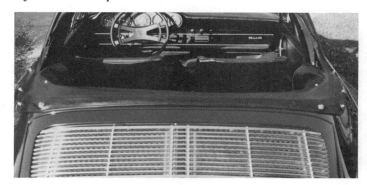

Soft window down with boot in place

A rare 1968 fixed window 1968 Targa

1972 Targa, note decal and defogger wires

As a final note of interest, on 1970 and 1971 models a decal showing a silver engine with a large orange "2.2" emblazoned on it was found on the inner surface, lower center of the rear glass on both coupe and Targa.

2.2 decal announced the first of many 911 displacement increases

Rear Wiper

A rear wiper was optional on coupes and Targas (with glass rear windows) built prior to 1969. When they first appeared is complicated by the parts manuals showing parts that would enable all cars to have them retrofitted. The fact that changes in parts to fit the rear wiper to cars built before chassis numbers 305 101, 354 001 and 458 101 (1967 model year break), implies that they were first offered for 1967 911 and 912 models. LHD wipers parked on the left side, while RHD versions parked on the right. Arms were available in silver or black, presumably linked to the color of the front arms.

Rear wiper, 1967 911S

Rear wiper motor and linkage, 1967 911S

Rear wiper, 1973 911 Targa (not U.S.-spec.)

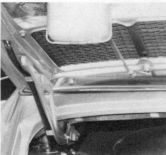

Rear wiper linkage, 1973 Targa

By 1969, the sole color was black for wiper blade and arm. The blade was unchanged from the previous version, as was the majority of the wiper assembly except the wiper arm. Again, the wiper was the same for coupe and Targa and different versions were available for RHD and LHD. No additional changes occurred between 1969 and 1973.

Rear Lid

The rear ventilation grille for the engine lid was identical on 911 and 912, coupe and Targa. The rear grille was modified during the early 1968 model year at chassis numbers 11 800 379, 11 805 122, 11 810 290, 11 820 368, 11 830 260, 11 850 118, 11 855 030, 11 860 107, 11 870 093, 11 880 064, 12 820 159, 12 870 337 and 12 801 832. This change corresponds to the change in rear lid which resulted in the disappearance of the center bar below the grille. The fastening hardware for these first two grilles was a peculiar aluminum T-bolt prone to failure due to weakness caused by corrosion. A wire mesh painted black and mounted to the lower surface of the grille prevented objects that could fit between the grille's bars from entering the engine compartment.

Rear grille, 1967 912, note satin black area under grille

Rear grille, 1968 911L with "barless" rear lid

The next version of the rear grille was fitted in 1969 only. It is subtly different from the one used in 1970-71. Both had flatter bars than the earlier version, the same black mesh screen and mounted identically with the same "cheese head" screws. There were three vertical straps on the 1969 version, while the later grille had five. A final rear grille type was used for 1972 and

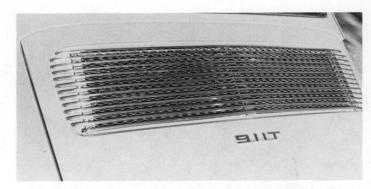

1969 rear grille, note central and outer straps

1973. It was identical to the previous version except in color. Anodized black replaced silver and a 2.4 or 2.7 insignia embellished the right hand side, depending upon what lived underneath.

Rear grille 1970-71, note 5 straps

Rear grille, 1972-73

Below the rear grille on 912s only was a plate to deflect water from the engine and generator. When it was first fitted is a bit obscure. The parts manual page

Deflector plate 912

30

that illustrates it is dated 3/67. The text indicates that it can be fitted to all cars from engine number 742 480 and 831 749, which corresponds to an early 1966 model year change. What is not stated is that it was fitted to these cars; it only states that it could be, which implies that it was not fitted. Its purpose was to keep water from directly striking the exposed generator and distributor.

A variety of other insignias graced the rear deck. We will start with the Porsche scripts and then proceed to the engine designation scripts.

A two-piece (that looks like a one piece) script bearing the name Porsche was found on the first 911 and 912 models. On 911s it was gold anodized aluminum and on 912s bright anodized aluminum. The appearance of the script was similar to the one used on the rear of 1962 and later 356 models, only larger. At the 1967 model change, chassis number 305 101 (911) and 354 971 (912), this script changed to six individual letters. The colors remained the same, gold and silver, with the new 911T, introduced in 1968, having the silver set.

Two piece Porsche script and angled model designation

For 1969 a part number change occurred, but no significant change is obvious. Gold letters were used on 911E and 911S models while 912 had silver (aluminum). The 911T came standard with silver letters, gold being optional. This continued until the 1972 model year when letters on all models became black. The only difference for 1973 was no Porsche name on the Carrera rear lid.

Engine designation scripts were found on all but the earliest 911s. The first angled 911 script was gold anodized to match the Porsche script. It was on the lower right corner of the rear lid. It was mounted by two pins 53mm apart. At some point not defined by the parts books, this script was modified to one mounted by two pins 46mm apart. No other change was made. 912s had corresponding changes with the 912 script finished in bright anodized aluminum to match the

Porsche script on these models.

For the 1967 model year the location of the script on both 911 and 912 moved up above the Porsche letter set to a central location below the rear grille; the color matched the letter set. These were "straight" as opposed to angled. There was also the addition of the 911S designation on appropriate models, also with gold finish. In 1968 there were two new engine types that were addressed. These were 911T (aluminum or optional gold) and 911L (gold). The others, 912, 911 and 911S remained as they were. In addition, a decal set was offered for the limited-production 911R. No other parts for this model, such as the altered signal units and plexiglas windows can be found in the parts manuals.

911R decal set

There were four models for 1969. These were 911S, 911E, 911T and 912. The first three insignias were available in gold (911T optional) and 911T and 912 in aluminum finish. 1970 and 1971 had the same combinations with the exception of the 912, which didn't make the cut in 1970.

The 1972 and 1973 models included 911T, 911E, 911S and Carrera. The first three now featured scripts bearing the engine designation in black anodized aluminum located in the same place as their earlier compatriots. Carreras presented another problem. A Carrera RS insignia is listed in the parts book. Included in the description are the words "not on rear lid with spoiler". This is puzzling since Carreras came standard with rear spoilers. Two other scripts are listed, one black and one matte gold. These were decals rather than raised insignias and bore the word "Carrera" only. There were also decals used on rear lids on the special models that were painted Grand Prix White. The decals read "Porsche" and "Carrera RS". They were available in blue, red, green or black.

In 1968 there first appeared an optional semi-automatic transmission known as the Sportomatic. It was still necessary to shift, but use of a clutch pedal was not necessary. It was comparable to the VW "Automatic Stick Shift". A raised script bearing the name, "Sportomatic" was on vehicles so equipped from 1968

Carrera decals   *Raised Carrera scripts*

SWB European-spec. tail light

through 1971. It was either gold or bright anodized aluminum depending on the other scripts on the car and was mounted directly below the engine designation script.

Rear Lights

Changes in the rear lights mirrored those of the front turn signal units. The first cars off the assembly line in Zuffenhausen had Bosch tail light units with non-removable lenses, chrome metal rims and white spongy seals. There were three varieties. The U.S. type had red lenses for turn indicator, reflector area and brake and tail light areas. The back-up light area had a clear lens. For Europe, there was an amber turn signal, a clear back-up lens, and red was used for reflector area and brake and tail lights. A third unit was made for French specification cars with a yellow lens for the back-up light.

The body change in 1969 necessitated a change in rear light unit. Also made by Bosch, these featured removable lenses, vacuum-metalized "rims" and black rubber seals. U.S.-version lights had reflectors incorporated into the side of the light, eliminating the need for the body-mounted reflectors tacked on in 1968. European cars got units with colors described above and without side reflectors. None of these tail light units incorporated rear reflectors. A separate rectangular reflector unit, also made by Bosch, was mounted on the rear bumper next to the bumperette on all mod-

els. These lights were used from 1969 through 1972. For 1973, the "rim" color of the lens changed to black but the light units were otherwise identical. The reflectors were unchanged.

LWB tail light with chrome trim, note also reflector   *1973 tail light lenses had black trim. This is a European lens*

Two small rectangular license lights were mounted in the inner structure of the rear lid. They were not modified from 1965 through 1973.

License lights lived in the rear lid

Rear fog lights became optional in 1969 for 911 and 912 models not intended for delivery to Italy, Switzerland, Sweden, Finland and, of course, the U.S. These were mounted to the right of the left bumper guard on the license panel. They remained optional through 1973.

SWB U.S.-spec. tail light unit

Rear Bumpers

Changes in the rear bumpers mirrored those of the front. The aluminum and vinyl decorative molding was identical to the front bumper trim, at least in cross section. The moldings, used on left and right halves were interchangeable. The 1965 through 1966 cars all used the same molding. The 1967 and 1968 911S and 1968 911L models (optional) used the wider S-trim molding as described on page 18. Other 1967 and 1968 models used the early style.

Standard trim with shrinking vinyl on the SWB bumper

Stainless steel cap on SWB bumper

1967 911S, note muffler skirt

For 1969 a change was dictated by the shortening of the bumpers and the addition of rear reflectors between the molding and the bumper guard. This difference

LWB bumper on 1969 912, note plain guard

was only in length from the earlier SWB versions although the leading ends of the S trim are slightly more beveled. The 912 and 911T in 1969 and the 911Ts of 1970 and 1971 used the standard molding, while 1969 through 1971 911E and 911S models used the S-type trim.

Trim cap on LWB bumper, note beveled end on S-trim

The S-trim moldings were unchanged for 1972 and 1973, except those fitted to the Carrera, which were different due to the rear flares. S-trim was standard on 911E and 911S and optional on the 911T.

The bumper guards, or bumperettes, flanking the license plate on all 911s and 912s were similar in appearance to the front bumper guards. The first cars had chrome guards with no rubber protective strips. Left and right sides were interchangeable. A page in the parts book dated 6/67 lists an optional part which is described as "Bumper horns rear for ram protection". This ram protection took the form of a single tubular chrome bar that was mounted between the bumper guards at the top edge. A rubber covering for the bumper guards was also listed as a separate part. By 1968 the rubber-covered variety got a different part number and became optional equipment.

In 1969 and 1970 the plain chrome guard was standard on 912 and 911T models, while the rubber covered variety came standard on 911E and 911S and was optional on the others. The "ram protection" bar continued to be optional on all models. For 1971 things were much the same except that ram protected rear bumpers with rubber coverings could not be had. Either could be ordered as an option, but not both on the same car. In 1972 the 911E got the same treatment as the 911T for 1971. The 911T and 911S were the same as their 1971 counterparts.

Two plastic caps cover the mounting bolts on the rear bumper guard

U.S.-spec. 1973 rear bumper guard

In markets outside the U.S., 1973 rear bumper guards were the same as 1972. The new Carrera shared the same equipment as the 911S and had the option of the ram protection bar. U.S. cars got their own form of ram protection with synthetic rubber bumper guards similar to those used up front. These were not identical twins but instead were mirror image.

An optional, three-piece stainless steel muffler skirt was first offered for 1968 models. It continued to be available through 1973. It was mounted below the rear bumpers and license panel.

Stainless steel muffler skirt first offered in 1968. The chrome bars are an aftermarket accessory not the ram protection original equipment option which had only a single protruding upper tube

Wheels and Hub Caps

The first 911 and 912 models featured the same type of slotted steel wheels found on 356Cs. They were finished in either silver metallic paint or chrome plated (optional). Width was 4 1/2" and diameter 15". These came with a nearly flat stainless steel hub cap with a "tarnished chrome" crest in the center. An enameled crest was optional.

4 1/2" x 15" painted steel wheel. Hub cap has "tarnished chrome" crest

Optional 4 1/2" x 15" chrome wheel

In 1967 the forged alloy Fuchs wheel, which was standard on the 911S and optional on other models, first appeared. For the 1967 model year these alloy wheels were 4-1/2" x 15"; however, by the 1968 model year, they were replaced by a wider 5-1/2" version. The alloy wheel featured an aluminum crested center cap secured by three clips. Also in the 1968 model year, 5-1/2" x 15" steel wheels appeared, replacing the 4 1/2" versions as standard equipment.

For 1969 through 1971 steel wheels were available painted silver or optionally chrome plated and only in 5-1/2" width. This chrome wheel was optional on all models. The hub cap was the same one used on earlier cars, but the enameled crest was no longer available. 6" x 15" alloy wheels were standard on 911S models, with a 5-1/2" x 14" alloy wheel found on 911E models. Optional on the 911T was a cast magnesium wheel with 5-1/2" x 15" dimensions. This ten spoke wheel was actually the lightest weight wheel that had ever been fitted to a production model. The 5-1/2" x 14" Fuchs wheel was fitted to 911Ts with the optional hydo-pneumatic front suspension. By 1971, 911Ts were fitted with any of the alloy wheel options.

The 4 1/2" x 15" Fuchs wheel fitted standard on the 1967 911S

5 1/2" x 15" chrome wheel with enameled hub cap crest

The 5 1/2" x 15" Fuchs wheel fitted standard on the 1968 911S

The 5 1/2" x 14" Fuchs wheel fitted standard on the 1969-71 911E

For 1972 and 1973 the chrome steel wheel was deleted. The standard wheel on 911T was 5-1/2" x 15" painted steel wheel, while the 1972 911E had a 6" x 15" wheel, optional on other models. On 1973 911E models the standard wheel was the cast aluminum "cookie cutter" wheel made by ATS, which was op-

The magnesium 5 1/2" x 15" 911T wheel used 1969-72

The 6" x 15" Fuchs wheel fitted standard on the 1969-73 911S

The ATS "cookie cutter" wheel appeared in 1973

The 7" x 15" Fuchs wheel was used on the 1973 Carrera at the rear

tional on 911Ts. It had the same dimensions as the previous steel wheel. The 6" x 15" alloy wheel was standard on the 911S and optional on other models. The 1973 Carrera had rear wheels 7 inches wide. Hub caps on all wheel types remained unchanged.

LUGGAGE COMPARTMENT

The principle occupants of the luggage compartment, aside from occasional luggage, are the spare tire, fuel tank, various electrical components, the ventilation system, the optional gas heater and the tool kit. Since spare tires were not particularly dynamic, and such things as collapsible spares did not occur until 1973, suffice it to say that they were there.

Fuel Tank

Fuel tanks on all 911 and 912 models were fundamentally the same and were located and mounted in the same manner. They all had filler necks mounted in the left front fender, and fuel exited to the engine from the lower rear center of the tank. A number of variations on the theme were present due to mechanical changes, changes in fuel pumps and evaporation chambers, all of which would, in most cases, cause some limitations in attempting to fit a non-original fuel system, although the tank would likely interchange with little difficulty. It is possible and indeed likely that a number of cars out there lack the proper complement of hoses and filters and plastic bottles and chambers.

The standard capacity of the fuel tank was 62 litres or approximately 16.4 U.S. gallons. They were painted grey. In mid-1965 the finish was changed to a textured coating, also grey in color. A larger, black-painted 100-litre (26.4 gallon) tank was optional starting in October 1966 (1967 model year). With the standard fuel tank, the spare tire fit in a well toward the front of the tank. This well was not present with the larger tank, so the spare sat on top of the tank and had a cover over it made of felt-type carpet material.

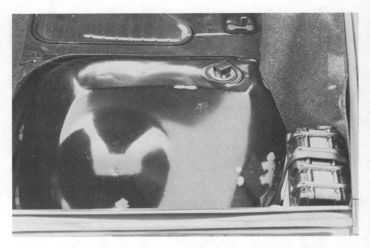

Optional 100 litre fuel tank, 1967 911S. Round impression located spare wheel. Note bracket at upper left where leather spare tire strap was anchored

Spare wheel, 1967 911S. Note leather strap, another 356 holdover

There were only two changes in the tank itself. At the 1969 model year both the 62 and 100-litre tanks were modified. The 100-litre tank was not available in the U.S. for 1969 and 1970 and completely disappeared at the 1971 model year. For 1973 a larger 85-

Fuel tank and luggage area, 1965 911. Grey painted tank. Battery can be seen at right

The fuel tank on 1969-72 cars was similar to the SWB tank at the left. Note windshield washer reservoir and incomplete ventillation system

1973 non-U.S. 911. Note 85-litre fuel tank, collapsible spare, lack of fuel tank ventilation system and washer reservoir filler in nose panel

litre (22.5 gallon) tank became standard equipment in all models except the 911T, for which it was optional. 911T models with Bosch K-Jetronic fuel injection had as standard a slightly altered version of the 62-litre tank. The electrical fuel level sending unit was identical on all tanks except the 100-litre tank, which due to the size and shape required a different sender.

From 1970 through 1973 a wonderful fuel tank ventilation system was developed for U.S. specification cars. A schematic is shown in illustration 2/1/2 in the 1970 parts book. No fundamental changes occurred through 1973.

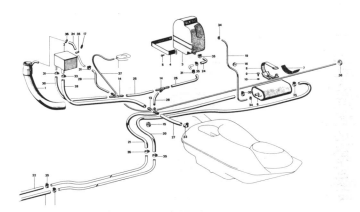

Illustration 2/1/2, 1969 Parts Book

Electrical Things

The items covered in this area include battery and associated hardware and fuse blocks. Wiper motors were discussed on page 23. The ventilation system with associated blowers will be covered next.

The 1965 through 1968 911 and 912 models used a single 12 volt battery, which was located in the left front part of the luggage compartment. The battery sported a plastic cover and sat in a plastic tray. It was held in place by a rubber strap, which hooked to a bracket on the front tank support.

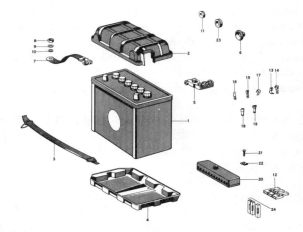

Illustration 9/2, 1965-68 Parts Book

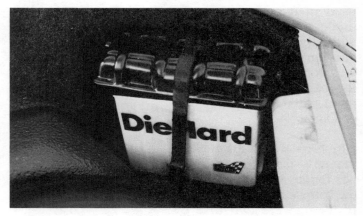

Battery complete with cover and strap, SWB 912

The 1969 912 had the same battery arrangement as the earlier cars. 911s, on the other hand, featured tandem 12-volt batteries wired in parallel. These were located in wells in the inner front fenders toward the front and held in place by metal straps. The 912 had the dual wells, although they were empty. No additional changes were made through 1973.

The ground cable and positive battery terminals follow the same progression as batteries with the only change occurring at the 1969 model year. In addition to these parts changing, there were also twice as many on the later cars due to the tandem battery arrangement.

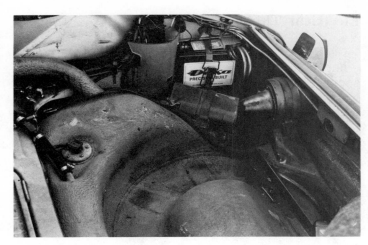

The batteries on LWB cars were mounted in the front inner fenders. Note fuel tank ventilation components. Conical shaped housing in front of the tank is part of the air conditioner and the reason the washer reservoir was relocated on cars so equipped

Both batteries on these cars were fitted with identical ground straps and positive terminals. A positive battery cable connected the two batteries and was routed around the rear of the fuel tank.

The fuse block on early 911s and 912s contained 12 fuses and appeared very much like the unit used in the 356, being made of black plastic with slightly domed top and curved corners. It was located up toward the back of the instrument panel on the driver's side.

SWB fuse block

In 1969 the fuse block moved to the left front inner fender behind where the battery lived. Actually, there were two fuse blocks; one containing ten fuses and one containing eight. These remained unchanged through the 1973 model year, although the wiring did not.

LWB fuse blocks

The luggage compartment was illuminated by lights which mounted on the rear corners of the inner structure of the front lid. Owners of some 911s and all 912s were not so fortunate receiving only one light unit and on the other side had a flat blanking plate. Through 1968 all 911s have two lights while 912s have a light on the left side only. For 1969 both 912 and 911Ts

Luggage compartment light mounted to the hood inner structure

Black plastic blanking plate secured by white plastic rivets

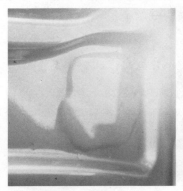

Unpunched hole, 1972-73 911

Right hinge held switch for luggage light. Protruding bracket below kept lights off when lid was closed

had the left side light only. 1970 and 1971 again featured two lights. On cars without both lights the blanking plates were grey cardboard and held on by phillips screws on 1965 and 1966. From 1967 through 1969 they were black plastic and held on by white plastic rivets. In 1972 and 1973 there was a light only on the right side and the "hole" on the left side was not punched, although a vestigial impression is obvious. On all cars the switch was on the right side hinge.

Ventilation System

Behind the fresh air vent on the cowl of the 1965 through 1968 911 and 912 was a valve controlled by a plastic lever on the dashboard. When open, fresh air entered the cockpit though a vent in the center of the dash top directed upward. When closed it did not, or at least it wasn't supposed to. . . A small fiberglass trough directed water, which entered this vent, to harmlessly drain out through the trunk floor. An optional forced air blower was available by the 1966 model year. It was in the well where the gas heater was located, if no gas heater was present.

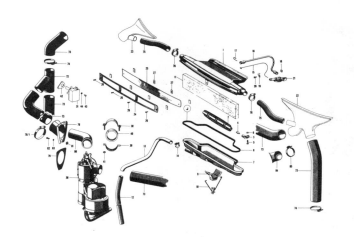

Illustration 2/3, 1965-68 Parts Book

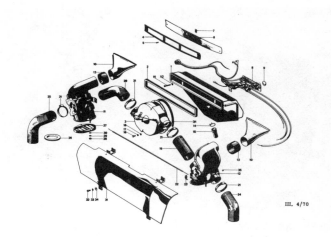

Illustration 9/8, 1972 Parts Book

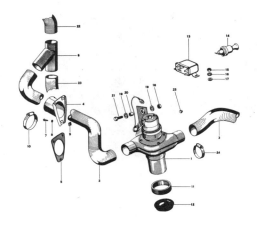

Illustration 2/5, 1965-68 Parts Book showing optional fresh air blower

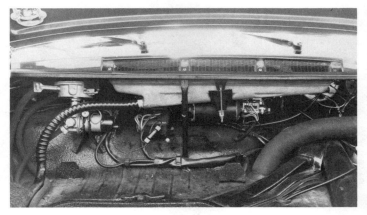

SWB ventilation system, note electric fuel pump for gas heater on left and wiper motor in the center

In 1969 a much revised ventilation system was found in the same location under the cowl. All models now enjoyed forced air ventilation for both fresh air and heat. Heated air came up to the cowl area from the engine via the longitudinals. At the same time fresh air came in through the vent in the cowl. The fresh air fan was mounted to the ductwork for the fresh air intake. A three lever system in the cockpit controlled everything.

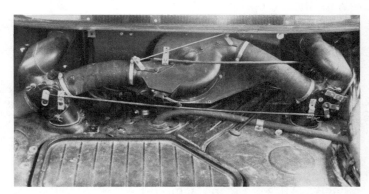

Ventilation system, normally hidden by a fiberboard partition, 1969-73

The top lever controlled the amount of fresh air allowed through the vent, much like the lever did on the earlier cars. Beyond the maximum opening were the three blower settings, which only worked with the fresh air vent wide open. Two plastic valves controlled the direction of the air flow, either up to the defroster or down on the front seat occupant's feet. The center lever controlled the direction of the fresh air, and the lower lever the direction of the heated air. Through careful manipulation it was possible to direct heated air forced by the blower onto either the windshield, drivers feet or both. This somewhat complicated device was hidden away from the rest of the luggage compartment by a fiberboard partition.

The three lever control directed air flow, hot or cold, up or down

Fresh air blower in the well where the gas heater lived, 1969-73

With the exception of the fresh air box, which was different for right-hand drive models, no changes were made from 1969 through 1972. In 1973, this air box was modified.

Gas Heater

Gasoline heaters were fitted as optional equipment on left-hand drive cars from 1965 through 1973. It was standard equipment on LHD 1966 911 and 1967 911S models. All were manufactured by Webasto, looked about the same and had the same basic structure. The earliest one described in the parts manual is noted as having a motor manufactured by AEG. This was used until December 1, 1965, although no chassis number cut off is noted.

The well where the gas heater was located. Note brake master cylinder reservoir on right

The second type is described as being equipped with a Bosch motor. The only visual difference from the outside was in the motor housing, shaped differently in order to accommodate the larger motor. This variation was used from the cessation of the previous type until chassis numbers: 308 069, 462 712, 500 420 and 550 272, corresponding to a late 1967 change. The parts book page is dated 6/67.

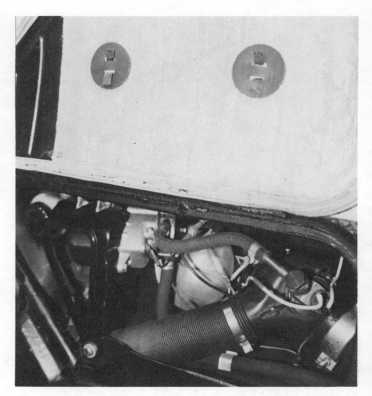

The gas heater in its lair. Note insulation panel on lid

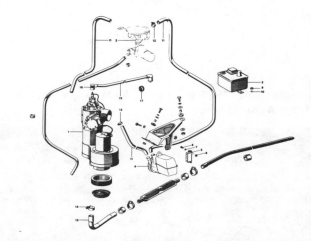

Illustration 2/3a, 1965-68 Parts Book

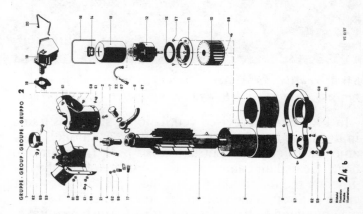

Illustration 2/4b, 1965-68 Parts Book showing all you ever wanted to know about gas heaters

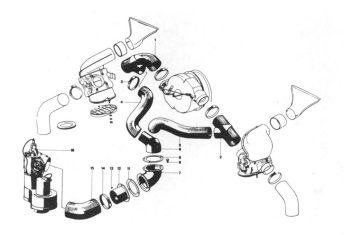

Illustration 0/9/2, 1972 Parts Book

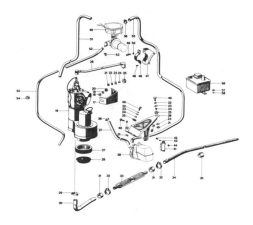

Illustration 0/9/2, 1972 Parts Book

The final type used in SWB cars is described with no particular mention of motor type, although from the illustration it seems to be of the Bosch variety. The outward difference on this model was the different spark box and temperature regulator. It was used from the chassis numbers listed above throughout 1967 and all of 1968.

The LWB version was again different in the temperature regulator at the top of the combustion chamber. This was the final permutation of the gas heater through 1973.

Right-hand steering cars were never equipped with gas heating units due to the substantially different inner structure of the luggage compartment floor.

Windshield Washer System

All 911 and 912 models came equipped with windshield washers. The nozzles are described on page 23. The first production cars featured a washer bag in the right inner fender with the neck protruding into the luggage compartment. This system was used up until

The washer reservoir was mounted in the right inner fender up to mid-1965

chassis number 302 694, 351 292 and 451 373 which corresponds to mid-1965, when the front shock absorber mounts became adjustable.

The new version consisted of a white hard-plastic windshield washer reservoir that mounted entirely in the luggage compartment. It was rectangular in shape and mounted inside the inner nose panel on the left side.

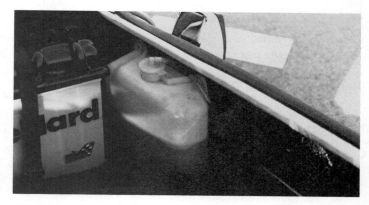

The second type of reservoir was mounted under the inner nose panel and somewhat difficult to fill

The final reservoir type was introduced for the 1968 model year and used through 1973. It was mounted inside the inner nose panel with its filler neck located to the left of the lower part of the front hood latch. For 911s fitted with air conditioning, built between the years 1969 through 1973 the reservoir was located in the upper left side of the luggage compartment. This was due to the air conditioner condenser which was on the floor of the luggage compartment (photo page 38).

All models, 1965 through 1973, used the same clear plastic washer tubing, the same white plastic "T" fittings and the same washer pump. The pump was controlled by the stalk on the right side of the steering column. The pump was located under the right hood hinge on early cars with the fender mounted reservoir, moving to the inner nose area when the reservoir

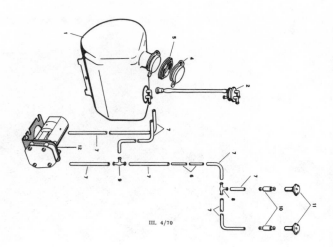

III. 4/70

Illustration 9/5, 1971 Parts Book showing the LWB washer reservoir pump and plumbing

Front latch panel with hole where reservoir was mounted to the right of the latch mechanism

moved that direction.

Carpeting

The items previously described were well hidden from the casual observer by carpeting, which blanketed the entire luggage area. The first cars came with carpeting much like that in 912 and 356 models, was a square weave loop-type carpet as opposed to the plush or "velour" carpeting used in the interior of the 911. It is referred to as Bouclé in the parts manuals. There were three pieces of trunk carpeting, including one piece that made up the floor and back wall and two side pieces. The side pieces were secured in place by glue. The main floor piece stayed in place by its own weight, although at the back, leather straps held it up. This piece had a heavy fiber backing glued to it. The carpet was bound on the edges with vinyl. At the time that the windshield washer bottle moved inside in mid-1965, all three carpet pieces were modified. This change also corresponded to the addition of adjustable shock mounts which were left uncovered so that adjustments could be made easily.

A second type of carpet material was also used on SWB cars called Perlon. It was a nylon material look-

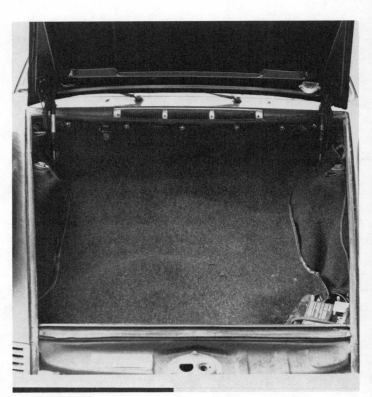

1966 911 with square weave or Bouclé carpeting

ing much like felt. It was less than one quarter inch thick and had a "pressed" look to it. It is not clear when this material was introduced, although it is certain that it was used on 911S models and all Targas. This would mean that it was definitely available in 1967 but was not necessarily exclusive to coupes. By 1968, this was the only material utilized. There was also a change noted in 1968 for left side wall and main floor section. A different floor section was used for cars fitted with the optional 100-litre fuel tank. These cars also had a spare tire covering of this material. In all other cars the tire resided below the floor carpeting.

Leather strap which holds the main floor section in place

For 1969 things changed. A fourth, front piece was found glued to the inside of the inner nose covering the washer bottle. The main floor piece attached at the rear by snaps rather than straps. Side pieces also attached by snaps. The snaps on the body were on little plates secured by the fender bolts. Perlon material was used exclusively, that is until 1972 when the parts manual lists the front piece in "velour" standard issue on 911S and 1973 Carrera with it being optional on 911E. It is interesting to note that none of the other three pieces were available in this material. No other changes occurred between 1969 and 1973.

Luggage compartment 1967 911S. Note lower ill-fitting Perlon carpeting and leather tire strap

Inner surface of luggage compartment mat. Note wood reinforcement

The snap which mounted the side and rear carpeting in the luggage compartment

Tool Kits

Tool kits are well documented for 911 and 912 models. The early 911 kit (1965 through 1968) consisted of:

Bag
Spark Plug Wrench with Pin
19 mm Wheel Nut Wrench
8 x 9 mm Open-end Wrench
10 x 11 mm Open-end Wrench
12 x 13 mm Open-end Wrench
14 x 15 mm Open-end Wrench
17 x 19 mm Open-end Wrench
19 x 22 mm Box Wrench
Screwdriver
Phillips Screwdriver
Pliers
Fan belt
Tire Gauge

1972 911, note windshield washer reservoir upper right

Plastic Bag with 5 Fuses
Fan Belt Wrench
Bottle of Glycerine
Allen Wrench for Oil Drain Plug
Jack

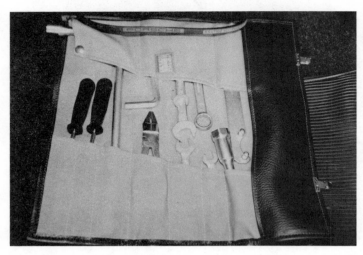

1965-68 911 tool kit

1965 through 1968 912 kits contained the following:

Bag
Spark Plug Wrench with Pin
19 mm Wheel Nut Wrench
8 x 9 mm Open-end Wrench
10 x 11 mm Open-end Wrench
12 x 13 mm Open-end Wrench
14 x 15 mm Open-end Wrench
17 x 19 mm Open-end Wrench
Screwdriver
Phillips Screwdriver
Pliers
Fan belt
Tire Gauge
Plastic Bag with 5 Fuses
Fan Belt Wrench
Bottle of Glycerine

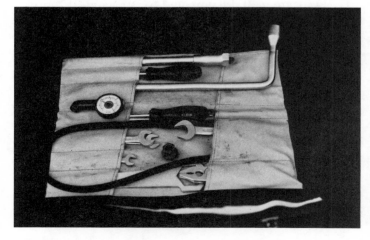

1965-68 912 tool kit

Lug Nut
Jack

1969 and 1970 911 kits contained the following:

Bag
Spark Plug Wrench with Pin
19 mm Wheel Nut Wrench
8 x 9 mm Open-end Wrench
10 x 11 mm Open-end Wrench
12 x 13 mm Open-end Wrench
14 x 15 mm Open-end Wrench
17 x 19 mm Open-end Wrench
19 x 22 mm Box Wrench
Screwdriver
Phillips Screwdriver
Pliers
Fan belt
Plastic Bag with 5 Fuses
Fan Belt Wrench
Allen Wrench for Oil Drain Plug
Jack

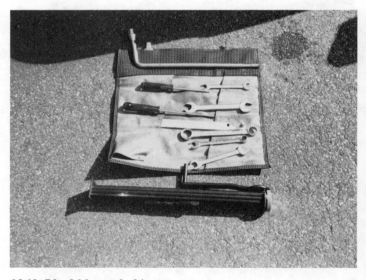

1969-70 911 tool kit

1969 912 kits contained the following:

Bag
Spark Plug Wrench with Pin
19 mm Wheel Nut Wrench
8 x 9 mm Open-end Wrench
10 x 11 mm Open-end Wrench
12 x 13 mm Open-end Wrench
14 x 15 mm Open-end Wrench
17 x 19 mm Open-end Wrench
Screwdriver
Phillips Screwdriver
Pliers
Fan belt
Plastic Bag with 5 Fuses
Fan Belt Wrench, 36 mm
Bottle of Glycerine
Jack

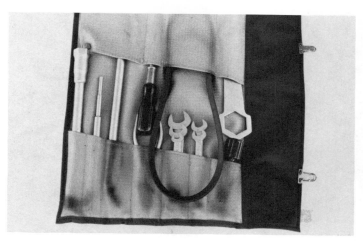

1969 912 tool kit

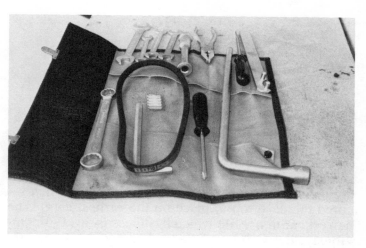

1971-73 tool kit

1971 through 1973 911 kits contained the following:

Bag
Spark Plug Wrench with Pin
19 mm Wheel Nut Wrench
8 x 9 mm Open-end Wrench
10 x 11 mm Open-end Wrench
12 x 13 mm Open-end Wrench
14 x 15 mm Open-end Wrench
17 x 19 mm Open-end Wrench
19 x 22 mm Box Wrench
Screwdriver
Phillips Screwdriver
Pliers
Fan belt
Plastic Bag with 5 Fuses
Fan Belt Wrench
Allen Wrench for Oil Drain Plug
Jack

INTERIOR

Dash Top

The dash top on the earliest cars was a padded vinyl affair constructed in one piece. The speaker for the optional radio was located in the center close to the windshield as evidenced by the perforations from which the sound escapes. Not mentioned in the parts manuals are the four screws covered by plastic caps which secured the dash top in place on the earliest cars. The newest car in my file which has these is 301175. Obviously, the RHD cars had a "mirror-image" corresponding part.

The almost mirror image RHD dashboard, 1967 911S. Note forward tunnel cover

Early dash top with "buttons"

Old and new, the 1968 911 dash top was used only one year

Dash top 1967, without buttons. Note radio plate

1969-on dashboard top

For the 1968 model year only, a unique combination of old and new two piece dashboard top was featured. The front portion was padded vinyl with speaker perforations as before. This was modified again in February 1968. The rear part, closest to the passengers, was a hard foam backed vinyl. Like the earlier version, you could have any color desired provided it was black.

From 1969 through 1973 the dash top once again became one piece. This version was all of the hard foam-backed vinyl, as the rear portion of the preceding type.

Replacing the speaker perforations was a separate speaker grille made of the same material as the dash top. This material was, unfortunately, prone to cracking following exposure to ultraviolet rays, heat and stress. The first place that seemed to be affected by these elements was

Speaker cover and omnipresent dashboard crack

46

toward the center next to the instrument pod. Again, only black was offered.

Instruments: 911

All 911s came fitted with five gauges. From 1965 through 1967 they had chrome bezels and black faces with green lettering. Starting in 1968, the bezels became black, while lettering changed from green to white; this combination, black faces with white letters, remained through 1973. A change in seals eliminated the brackets securing the gauges from behind for the 1970 model year.

Starting left to right, one first encounters the fuel gauge. On the first 911s this was a combination instrument which also contained an oil level gauge. This particular gauge was used until chassis number 305-100 which corresponds to the end of the 1966 model year. A different instrument with similar appearance was designed for use with the optional 100-litre fuel tank. This gauge was used through the 1967 model year for the 911S model. Other 1967 911s had a fuel gauge without the oil level indicator. A giant low fuel warning light graced its bottom. There were two varieties depending on size of fuel tank.

Early dual scale fuel/oil level gauge, used on 911 only

This left gauge was used on 1967 912s and some 911s

1968 combination instrument with white lettering

1972 vintage combination instrument. Lettering is slightly different from gauge on left

In 1968 the white-on-black gauges first appeared. The fuel gauge contained the oil level indicator on the 911S and the U.S. specification 911L. Other models, including the European spec. 911L, had only a fuel level indicator. Instruments, once again, varied based on size of fuel tank.

For 1969, the combined instrument changed although its outward appearance was identical to the 1968 version. It was still fitted standard on the 911S and optional on the 911T and 911E. The standard fuel gauges for 911T and 911E were the ones used in 1968.

1970 brought with it the final change for this instrument. It was a change that consisted of the seal modification mentioned earlier. The single fuel gauge was standard on 911T through 1971 and standard on 911T and 911E in 1972 and 1973. The combination gauge was standard on other models and optional on those just mentioned. This instrument, in all configurations, was available only in a "German language" version.

The second gauge from the left was either a combination oil temperature/oil pressure or a single oil temperature gauge, depending on the model and options. The 1965 and 1966 model year 911s had a black faced gauge with green lettering. The left side scale had oil temperature in degrees and the right side was oil pressure which was measured in kp/cc. There were both German and English versions of this instrument. Two warning lights were found on this gauge. The upper light was white in color and was illuminated when the handbrake was in use. The lower red light was an alternator light.

For 1967 the 911S kept the combination gauge from 1966. All other models had only a temperature scale (without numbers) on the gauge. The latter gauge came in single language only because "temp" in German has the same connotation as "temp" in English. There were three warning lights on the single scale gauge. The left indicator was red in color and lights when the charging system was non-functional. The large lower light was white in color and signified handbrake in use. The final light, on the right, green in color signified lack of oil pressure.

1968 again was a change from green lettering to white. Like the small combination gauge described earlier, the 911S and the U.S. spec. 911L had the combination instrument, while other models had the temperature only version. Language on these gauges was as it was in 1967. A third version (German language only) of this combination instrument was used on all cars equipped with Sportomatic transmission. It had both oil temperature and pressure scales although the temperature scale had different numbers. Warning lights were the same as the previous versions.

The Sportomatic equipped 1969 sported the same

This gauge was used from 1965-67 on 911s

Temperature gauge used on 1967 912 and some 911s

Tachometer, 1965-67 911

Tachometer 1968-on 911

Combination instrument 1968 911L Sportomatic. Note 50-150 scale

Combination instrument 1968 911L with manual transmission. Note 60-140 scale

combination gauge as 1968, but the other two varieties changed with the addition of international symbols on the warning lights. The dual scale gauge was standard on the 911S and optional on other models. German and English versions were once again offered.

New symbols identified warning lights in 1969

1970 through 1973 911s shared the large combination gauge in the same fashion as the small instrument to its left. The dual scale gauge was standard on the 911S and Carrera and optional on all other models, which were fitted standard with the single scale temperature gauge. Sportomatics once more had their own versions. Warning lights were, again, as described for 1965 through 1967 cars.

The tachometer was the center and largest instrument of the five. The first version was used on all 1965 through 1967 911s with the exception of the 911S. The higher red line on the 911S was the only difference. The turn signal indicator lights and high beam indicator are located on the tachometer.

For the 1968 model year the lettering changed from green to white. Three tachometers with differing red lines were available. They were used for both 1968 and 1969. Since there was only one engine approved by the E.P.A., all U.S.-spec. cars had the same tach in 1968. This was the one that was fitted on the 911E of 1969. For the rest of the world, the 1968 911L was also so equipped. The 1968 911TU, which was not imported to the U.S. shared its tachometer with the 1969 911T, which was. 1968 and 1969 911S models shared tachs as well.

The 911 T, E and S models of 1970 had tachometers unique to that year, differing from the earlier version by the addition of the high beam symbol. By 1971 the tachometer made one final change, although the outward appearance of the instrument was identical. There were three versions, one each for the 911 T, E and S. The 1973 Carrera shared tachometers with the 911S. Tachometers came in a bilingual format UPM/RPM.

To the right of the tachometer was the speedometer. Only two black/green varieties existed between 1965 and 1967: one for miles per hour and the other for kilometers per hour. The 1968 and 1969 speedometers were white lettered and there was, once again, both a miles and kilometer type.

Speedometer, 1965-67 911

Speedometer, 1968 911S km/h type

The kilometer version for 1970 with new the style seal was the final type of kilometer speedometers. On the 1973 Carrera, a 10 - 300 km unit took the place of the standard 10 - 250 km speedometer. All miles units were 10 - 150. There was a change in the mile per hour unit in 1971 as well as the one in 1970. There were no further changes. All speedometers featured trip odometers as well as standard odometers. Trip odometers measured to the tenth of a mile/km and standard odometers measured to the mile/km. A small green light at the lower center indicated that the parking lights were on.

1972 M.P.H. speedometer

The fifth and final standard instrument was an electric clock which was the same size as the small combination gauge and located to the far right. The black/green clock was unaltered from 1965 to 1967. A change occurred for the 1968 through 1969 black/white version. 1970 and 1971 which featured the new seal type. A final change was made in 1972, although the face was unaltered. Time came only in one language.

Clock, 1965-67

Clock, 1968-73

Instruments, 912

Left to right is a little more difficult on the 912 since many cars did not come equipped with five instruments as did the 911. For those 1965 through 1966 912s which did have five gauges, as opposed to three, the furthest left was an ambient temperature gauge. Differing from the instrument listed in the next section, this one was 80-mm in diameter, which was the same size as the outer instruments in 911s. The diameter of the one which mounted in the lower dash was 60-mm. There was only one type available; it read in °C with a scale from -20 to 40 degrees.

For 1967 the outer instrument became standard. It was a fuel gauge very similar to the ones used in 1967 911s not fitted with 911S instruments. There were two versions, one for the 62-litre tank and one for the 100-litre tank. The lower part of the gauge had a large low fuel indicator (photo page 45).

The five gauge option on 1966 912s. Note ambient temperature gauge on left

For the 1968 and 1969 model years, all gauges went to black face with white lettering from the green lettering used previously. Aside from this there was no fundamental change. The same fuel gauge was used in 911 models without 911S instrument packages.

Second from the left on 1965 and 1966 912s with five instruments and on the left for cars with three was a combination fuel and oil temperature gauge. The 1967 version was only an oil temperature gauge. It was the same one used in 911s without S gauges. It also featured the same three warning lights (photo previous page).

1968 912 fuel gauge

Combination gauge, 1965-66 912

For 1968 the lettering went from green to white and, again, this instrument was shared with the 911s without S instruments. The 1969 version was different from the 1968 and again common to 911s of the same vintage.

The tachometer was central in position. From 1965 through 1967 green lettered versions were used. There was a slightly different face on 1967 models than the earlier tach. The 1968 and 1969 cars had white lettered versions. Warning lights for turnsignals and high beams were present.

To the right of the tachometer was the speedometer. These were differentiated from their 911 counterparts by their lack of expectation. The European version went to 200 kph with 120 mph on U.S. and British cars. A warning light for parking lights was at the

Tachometer, 1965-66

Tachometer, 1967, note different lettering

lower center.

The only change for this instrument was in 1968 when the lettering changed from green to white. Like the 911 unit, there was a separate trip odometer.

The instrument on the far right was the same clock used on similar vintage 911s.

1965-67 speedometer was less optomistic than the 911 version

Three central gauges, 1968 912. Note symbols on combination gauge

Optional Instruments

Ambient temperature gauges were offered as optional equipment on both 911 and 912. The 644 prefix on the part number hearkens back to the 356, which was also known to be so equipped. For the 1965 through 1967 period these gauges had black faces with green lettering. There were three varieties. Two had Celsius scales; these were made by VDO and Moto Meter. A third version, also made by Moto Meter, had a Fahrenheit scale.

In 1968, the last year for this option, lettering went to white, as with other gauges. The same three options were available in regard to scales and manufacturers. All of them functioned via a temperature probe mounted on the inner front fender. The placement of this 60-mm diameter gauge was to the left of the ignition switch on the only vehicles so equipped that I have seen.

Switches and Dashboard-Mounted Controls

Rather than address these part by part, it makes sense to group these year by year as most changes took place en masse. There will be three groupings: 1965 through 1968, 1969 through 1971 and 1972 and 73.

Through 1967 all dash mounted switches had knobs made from black hard plastic. The headlight switch had a plain, slightly dished, knob similar to the lighter knob, which was slightly smaller in diameter and shinier. For cars so equipped, the fog light switch had a small yellow illuminated center. The rear window defogger and four-way flasher used the same switch and knob but had a large illuminated red center. The gasoline heater control knob had a small illuminated red center. In 1967 the bases for the switches went from black to chrome.

1966 911 switch cluster without 4-way flasher

1966 911 with 4-way flasher mounted between the fog light and gas heater switch. Note black plastic base, large illuminated center and warning lable

1967 911 central switch cluster, note chrome bases

The 1968 model year brought rubber covers for the plastic knobs. There was no change in switches, just soft rubber covers which more than doubled the size of the knob. In the center of these covers was a plastic insert with a symbol which indicated the function of the switch. Some of centers, once again, were illuminated when the switch was in the on position. The sunroof switch used in 1965 through 1968 was the same switch used for electric windows, and was mounted below the instrument pod and above the ignition switch.

1968 switch cluster. Knob with propeller symbol on right is for the optional blower. The gas heater switch would have been in the same location, but the symbol on the knob looked like a stretched coil spring

1968 911 with rear window defogger. Note the wide ash tray handle and symbols on the steering column. The plastic lever under the clock is the fresh air (from cowl vent) control. The lighter has a VW knob (not original).

Shiny black lighter knob on 1967 911 dashboard. The knob below the speedometer is for the trip odometer. Note thin handle on ash tray

The ignition switch on 1965 through 1968 took two basic forms. For the U.S. and right-hand steering versions, a switch without a steering column lock was used, while the rest of the world received a switch combined with a column lock. The plastic rim, which retained the switch in place, was a small black affair for 1965 and early 1966 European delivery cars. The familiar wide black plastic "washer" that held the ignition switch in place was introduced mid-1965 for 911s without steering column lock. 912s received a peculiar small ring with thin washer through the 1966 model year. In 1967 all models were fitted with the wide washer.

1965 911 ignition switch

1965-66 912 ignition switch

1966-68 U.S.-spec ignition switch (without steering column lock). To the left is the headlight switch

European-spec. 1967 911S. Note ignition switch is column lock type

For 1969 through 1971 the same rubber covered knobs were used as on 1968 models. The headlight switch used in 1969 was the same as the one from 1968. For 1970 and 1971 a different switch was used. The four-way flasher switch was different from the one used in 1968 but still used the rubber knob type switch. The version used in 1970 and 1971 was considerably different. It consisted of a red translucent plastic push button. European and U.S. versions differed, presumably in language.

Push-button 4-way flasher switch first fitted in 1970. Note also lables over switches which were first used in 1972

A different fog light switch was used in 1969 and 1970 cars while yet another type was used in 1971. The first one is noted as being a two-position switch operating both front and rear fog lights. The lighter used in 1969 and 1970 was the same as the one used in 1968. A new lighter was used for 1971.

Dashboard 1969 911E. Central knob cluster left to right: fog light switch, lighter, rear window defogger. Note new ventillation control left of radio

Dashboard 1971 911T. Plastic plug fills hole where fog light switch would have been installed

Dashboard 1973 911. Rear window defogger on left followed by gap where fog light switch would be, if installed, and lighter on the right. To the left of the switches is a rectangular "fasten seat belts" warning light. The air conditioner installed is aftermarket

Two new switches were introduced in 1969 for the rear window defogger. One was a single position and the other was for the "two-stage" window. Two-stage was Porsche's way of describing that there were two heating levels. These were used through 1971. A new switch was also fitted for the gasoline heater in 1969 which was used through 1971. A new sunroof switch was also introduced in 1969 and used through 1971.

Ignition switches also changed for 1969. There are two types, one with steering lock and one without. No indication is provided regarding which cars were fitted with the non-locking model. The 1970 models were the first to use ignition keys with plastic-covered ends. The U.S.-specification cars came equipped with buzzers to let you know that your key was in the ignition when the door was open. There was no non-locking column ignition switch listed for 1970 and later. Switches were modified again for 1971.

The headlight switch was modified in 1972, and a different version was made for U.S.-spec cars. These were used in 1973 as well. The four-way flasher switches for 1972 were the same as those for 1971. New U.S. and European switches were fitted for 1973.

The 1972-73 fog light switch was the same one used in 1969-70, oddly enough not the one used in 1971. There was also a switch for cars fitted with rear fog light only. The lighter used in 1972 was the same one used in 1971. A different lighter was fitted in 1973.

Rear window defogger, gas heater and sunroof switches for 1972 and 1973 were unchanged from 1971. The ignition switches were, likewise, comparable to their 1971 counterparts.

Lower Dash Trim

The lower dashboard on 1965 and 1966 911 models was covered by a set of wood trim panels. This was actual wood veneer, as opposed to contact paper or plastic. The set consisted of five pieces. The piece on the left was different, depending on whether or not the ambient temperature gauge was fitted. At the time when the kneeguard wrapped upward around the edge of the dashboard, the wood trim changed. It was bordered top, bottom and back by a thin layer of aluminum. Since its ends were covered by upholstery, there was no need for the ends to be beveled, as they were in the earlier style, which did not have the aluminum backing. This change occurred between chassis number 301710 and 302243.

The first 912 models had painted dashboards that matched the exterior body. Later versions had a matte black finish, like the 911, but instead of the wood trim brushed aluminum was substituted. This type trim was also used on all other models in 1967 and 1968 except the 911S and 911 L models. The 1967 911S had a basket weave vinyl, while the 1968 911S and the 1968 911L had either the basket weave or an "elephant hide" type upholstery.

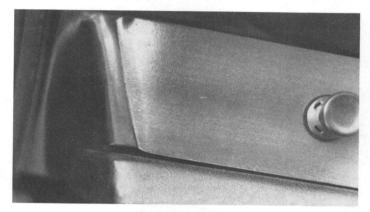

Early kneeguard with beveled wood which is not mounted in aluminum channel

Later style kneeguard and brushed aluminum lower trim are found on this 1967 912

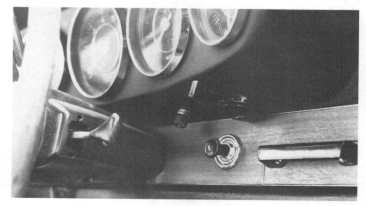

Wood trim set in metal channel. Note textured black paint on instrument pod

Early painted dashboard in 1965 912. Note radio plate. Steering wheel, supplemental gauges and fire extinguisher are not original

1967 911S with basket weave dashboard trim

"Elephant hide" dashboard trim, 1968 911L

1969 911s and 912s shared lower dash trim, which was then a basket weave black vinyl glued into a bright anodized aluminum frame. 1970 and 1971 had a nearly identical version.

1971 911T with basket weave lower dashboard trim. Aftermarket Cool-Aire air conditioner unit

A final version for 1972 and 1973 had the same aluminum frame with a leather grain vinyl. This did not have the basket weave texture used in the earlier cars. It was available in the following colors: black, tan and brown. It matched the vinyl on the door panels.

1973 911 dashboard trim. Also note plaid cloth seat inserts

With the exception of the very early production cars, all 1965 through 1971 cars carried their model designation on the right side of the glove box door in the form of a small script similar to the one located on the rear lid. In 1972 the model designation was removed. The glove box itself was always lockable. From 1967-70 the lock was offset slightly toward the car's center line. There was a small black plastic handle that opened the door through 1966. In 1967 the entire upper edge of the lid was modified to curve downward making the entire width the handle. The lock was centrally located in 1971 and the key lock was replaced by a rubber-covered lock knob that twisted to release. This is one of the few detail differences which differentiates 1970 from 1971 cars.

Script-less glovebox door. Scripts appeared about the time that the 912 was introduced

Angled engine designation script on glovebox door mirrored engine lid scripts mid-1965-66. Note plastic handle

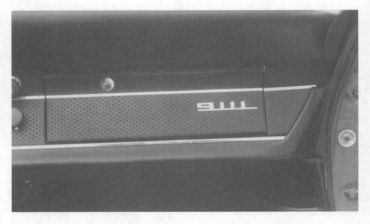

In 1967 the entire top edge of the glovebox door became the handle as seen on this 1968 911L

The upholstered knee guard panel made up the bottom part of the dashboard. From 1965 through 1968 this was a single piece, while 1969 through 1973 had left and right halves with the ash tray in the center.

The original straight style was used through mid-1965. For late 1965 the knee guard was modified on the ends to cover the ends of the dashboard, wrapping around and up to the top of the trim. On 911, 912 and 911TU (European 1968) the material used was the same as the 1966 and 1967 dash top and was padded

Scripts disappeared again in 1972. The central mounted twist knob replaced the glovebox key lock in 1971

in a similar fashion. This material type was used from 1965 through 1968 except on the 911S and 911L which used the hard foam backed vinyl used on later model dash tops.

For 1969 through 1973 the lower dash trim was three pieces, as mentioned above. The center section was the ash tray, which had moved down in position from its location in the SWB cars. All three pieces were black hard-foam-backed vinyl.

On cars with air conditioning, the interior vents were below the knee guard trim. The early version is illustrated in the 1968 parts book on a page dated 6/67. The first listing in the accessories manual is for 1967 and states that dealer installation in the U.S. was the only option. This unit was centrally located with controls on the left side. The left knob was the thermostat and the right side was the blower switch. In the accessories catalog it is referred to as "Porscheaire".

For 1969 through 1973 a different type air conditioner was offered. Although it was located in approximately the same location it was "split" in the center below the ash tray. It was manufactured by Behr, which made much of the fresh air ventilation system. They

were installed "out of house" following assembly at the Porsche factory. Those cars fitted with air conditioning had the windshield washer reservoir relocated to the upper part of the luggage compartment due to the front mounted condenser and evaporator unit. Controls were located toward the center of the car. On the left side was the temperature control and on the right was the blower control.

Temperature control on left and blower speed control on right. Ash tray in middle

Below the kneeguard on the left side was the front lid release. Originally a round knob was used. In 1969 the plastic T-handle used on the rear lid release replaced it.

A locking front hood release was available as an option. The first ones were a left over 356 part. On coupes this type was used through the 1968 model year. Targas, on which the locking release was standard, had a different mechanism. It was modified in mid-1968 at chassis numbers 11 850 036, 11 860 038, 11 855 002, 11 870 001, 11 880 002 and 12 870 037. A final revision for the 1969 model year allowed coupes and Targas to share the same device.

The Behr air conditioner fitted 1969-73, please ignore shift lever and equalizer

Locking front release, 1967 911S. Note carpeted strengthening rod

The plastic T-handle was used from 1969-on

Radio, Aerial

It should be noted that radios were optional equipment for 911 and 912 models. From 1965 through 1968 cars not so fitted came with a black plastic plate covering the radio opening. It bore the word Porsche in chrome letters etched into the back and was held in place by two round-headed rivets (photo see page 53).

1969 911 and 912 models without radios had a flat panel with black basket weave pattern vinyl. These were the first radio-less Porsches, since 1950 not to have a plate or a metal script with the word Porsche in the place where the radio was installed. 1970 and 1971 also had the same radio plate, while in 1972 and 1973 it matched the rest of the dash trim.

During this era many radios were dealer installed making many combinations of radios and aerials "original". The following listing are those radio types offered as optional equipment by the Porsche factory:

1965
Blaupunkt
Bremen, AM/LW
Stuttgart, AM/LW/SW
Frankfurt, AM/FM/LW
Frankfurt, AM/FM/LW (U.S. band)
Köln, AM/FM/LW signal seeking
Köln, AM/FM/LW signal seeking (U.S. band)
Becker
Monte Carlo, AM/LW
Europa, AM/FM/LW
Europa, AM/FM/LW (U.S. Band)
Mexico, AM/FM/LW signal seeking
Mexico, AM/FM/LW signal seeking (U.S. band)

1966
Blaupunkt
Bremen, AM/LW
Frankfurt, AM/FM/LW/SW
Frankfurt-US, AM/FM
Köln, AM/FM/LW signal seeking
New Yorker, AM/FM/SW signal seeking (U.S. band)
Becker
Monte Carlo, AM/LW
Europa, AM/FM/LW/SW
Europa, AM/FM (U.S. Band)
Mexico, AM/FM/LW signal seeking
Mexico, AM/FM/LW signal seeking (U.S. band)

1967
Blaupunkt
Bremen, AM/LW
Frankfurt, AM/FM/LW/SW
Frankfurt-US, AM/FM
Köln, AM/FM/LW signal seeking
New Yorker, AM/FM/SW signal seeking (U.S. band)
Becker
Monte Carlo, AM/LW
Europa, AM/FM/LW/SW
Europa, AM/FM (U.S. Band)
Grand Prix, AM/FM/LW signal seeking
Grand Prix, AM/FM signal seeking (U.S.band)

1968
Blaupunkt
Bremen, AM/LW
Boston, AM (U.S. band)
Frankfurt, AM/FM/LW/SW
Frankfurt-US, AM/FM
Köln, AM/FM/LW signal seeking
New Yorker, AM/FM/SW signal seeking (U.S. band)
Becker
Monte Carlo, AM/LW
Europa, AM/FM/LW/SW
Europa, AM/FM (U.S. Band)
Grand Prix, AM/FM/LW signal seeking
Grand Prix, AM/FM signal seeking (U.S.band)

1969
Blaupunkt
Bremen, AM/LW
Boston, AM (U.S. band)
Frankfurt, AM/FM/LW/SW
Frankfurt-US, AM/FM
Köln, AM/FM/LW signal seeking
New Yorker, AM/FM/SW signal seeking (U.S. band)
Becker
Monte Carlo, AM/LW
Europa, AM/FM/LW/SW
Europa, AM/FM (U.S. Band)
Grand Prix, AM/FM/LW signal seeking
Grand Prix, AM/FM signal seeking (U.S. band)
Philips
AM/LW cassette

1970
Blaupunkt
Hamburg, AM/LW
Boston, AM (U.S. band)
Frankfurt, AM/FM/LW/SW
Frankfurt-US, AM/FM
Köln, AM/FM/LW signal seeking
New Yorker, AM/FM/SW signal seeking (U.S. band)
Becker
Grand Prix, AM/FM/LW signal seeking
Grand Prix, AM/FM signal seeking (U.S.band)
Philips
AM/LW cassette

1971
Blaupunkt
Frankfurt-US, AM/FM

1971 (cont.)
  Blaupunkt
    Köln, AM/FM/LW signal seeking
  Philips
    AM/LW cassette

1972
  Blaupunkt
    Frankfurt, AM/FM/LW/SW
    Frankfurt-US, AM/FM
    Köln, AM/FM/LW signal seeking
  Becker
    Grand Prix, AM/FM/LW signal seeking
  Philips
    AM/LW cassette

1973
  Blaupunkt
    Ludwigshafen, AM/FM
    Frankfurt, AM/FM/LW/SW
    Frankfurt-US, AM/FM
    Lübeck CR, AM/FM cassette
    Bamberg, AM/FM/LW stereo
    Coburg, AM/FM/LW electronic
    Köln, AM/FM/LW signal seeking
  Becker
    Mexico, AM/FM stereo

Aerials were mounted on the front fenders when radios were installed. If a factory installation, manual aerials were on the left fender. Due to the size and gas filler left side mounting was not possible for the optional power antenna, so they were fitted to the right fender. Both manual and power aerials were manufactured by Hirschmann.

Changes were recorded in 1969 and 1972 for power aerials. Manual antennas were identical from 1965 through 1973.

Manual aerial mounted on the left front fender

Power aerial mounted on the right fender forward of the manual mounting point on the left

Steering Column

The two switches that shared the steering column of 911s and 912s were a turn signal/headlight dimmer on the left and a wiper/washer switch on the right. From 1965 through 1967, the flattened knobs were the same black plastic ones used on 356Bs and Cs. In 1968 the switches were modified with the main outward appearance change being the rubber knobs, which were similar in shape to the earlier plastic ones.

Shiny black hard plastic turnsignal and wiper knobs were used through the 1967 model year

In 1969 both switches changed, primarily because the wiring connections changed. More wiring changes in 1970 led to new switches again. For 1971 the turn signal switch remained the same as the 1970 version; the wiper switch reverted to the one used in 1969. The 1972 and 1973 models used the same wiper switch as in 1971, while the turn signal switch changed yet again. Knobs on all column switches from 1968 on were identical.

The rubber knob used from 1968-73 looked similar to the earlier knob. Note symbols

Corresponding to the early steering column switches was a black metal column housing. A plastic housing was substituted in 1968, complete with little international decals to tell you what the switches do. This housing remained unchanged through 1973. For 1972 and 1973 the decals changed on the wiper control for the U.S. market only the words "wash" and "wipe" were substituted for the symbols used on earlier cars.

Wash and wipe decals were for U.S.-bound cars only

Steering Wheel

The steering wheels in early 911 models were wood with four black painted horizontal spokes. The first version of this wheel had aluminum spokes, which were riveted to the center hub. In comparison to later wheels the wood used was lighter in color and the aluminum "spine" could be seen on the outer rim. The

Early style wood wheel with painted spokes and aluminum spine, note rivets

Later wood wheel with plastic coated spokes

later wheel had black plastic coated steel spokes, darker wood and a black stripe was painted around the front surface of the outer rim. The change is not documented by the parts manuals, but occurred mid-1965. Wood wheels were standard in 1965 and 1966. They were optional on 912s of the same era and on 1967 and 1968 911 and 912 models.

Standard on 912s and optional (no cost) on 911 was a black plastic-rimmed wheel, described as hard rubber and Ebonite in subsequent versions of the parts manuals. For 1967 and 1968 911S models the steering wheel was leather covered. This wheel was optional on other models. All wheels were 400 mm in diameter.

Plastic or "Ebonite" steering wheel, note horn pad

400 mm leather wheel was used from 1967-73

All three types above were also available in a "projecting hub" version which placed the steering wheel 30 mm (or about 1 1/4 inches) closer to the driver. These are listed as optional. The center of the steering wheel featured a horn contact. Early cars had a small round cover with an embossed Porsche crest on the leather center. A rectangular "butterfly" horn ring was introduced in 1965. It was listed as a no cost option for the 1966 911 and optional on 912. Both styles continued to be used through 1968. Construction was a metal casting, painted black with a leather center, again with the embossed Porsche crest.

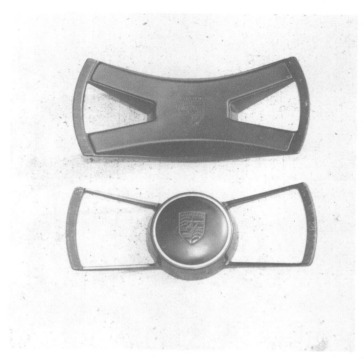

Late and early horn rings

For 1969 through 1971 the wood rimmed wheel was gone. The hard rubber and leather-covered wheels were modified but similar in appearance to the previous wheels. The wheels with "projecting hubs" were also still available as options on all models. The leather wheel was standard on 911E and 911S with it being optional on 911T and 912.

These four wheels made a return appearance for 1972. In 1973 there were three additional wheels, two of which are listed as having a "foamed" rim. These were replacements for the hard rubber rim standard on all models except the 911S and Carrera. The 911S came standard with the leather-rimmed wheel but could be fitted with optional projecting-hub types of wheel. The Carrera came standard with a leather rimmed 380 mm wheel.

380 mm Carrera leather steering wheel

All cars built between 1969 and 1973 used the same horn button, which was similar to the one introduced in 1967. These had a metal frame and were covered by a cushioned plastic described in the parts manuals as "artificial foam".

Sun Visors

The sun visors of 1965 and 1966 coupes were mirror image in shape and made from an off-white textured vinyl. On 911s the passenger's side came equipped with a vanity mirror. From 1965 through 1967 it was possible to order an optional driver's side visor with a vanity mirror. In 1966 this was a no cost option on 911s. Both mirrors were optional on 912s. These visors did not have a pivot to allow the visor to be moved to the side window.

Mirror-less visors, 1966 912

911s came standard in 1965-66 with this passengers side vanity mirror (optional on 912s)

Vanity mirror on the drivers side was a no cost option on 1965-66 911s

Visors on 1967 Targas were black on both sides

Pivoting viors, 1968 coupe, note light colored clips

Visors 1967 coupe, black when down, white when up

As in 1967, 1968 coupe visors were black down and white up

The late 1968 targa visors were subtly different than their 1967 counterparts

Visors used in 1969, note dark center clips

The next version introduced for the 1967 model year differed substantially. They were white on the side facing the windshield and black on the other side. They were again non-pivoting, mirror-image items. A different visor was used on Targas, which was entirely black. These types were used until just into the production of the 1968 model year at chassis numbers 11 800 147, 11 810 106, 11 820 004, 11 830 003, 11 805 000, 12 820 030 and 12 800 239 for coupes and 11 850 035, 11 860 037, 11 855 001, 11 870 000, 11 880 001 and 12 870 036 for Targas.

Following this type visor, coupes came fitted with the first pivoting visor that could be turned to the side. The sunvisors found in Targas, while different from their predecessor, did not feature the pivoting action. The visors on 1969 models were unique to that year following the same basic configuration of the 1968 type.

Visors, 1972

For 1970 through 1972, U.S. specification cars differed from their European counterparts. Mirrors were not fitted on U.S.-spec. cars. They were once again the same configuration as in 1968 and 1969. A final type was made for the 1973 model year. An optional left side visor was made specifically for the Carrera model.

Visors, 1973 Targa

Mirror

The rear view mirror was mounted in a central position between the sun visors. The first version was mounted by three screws, which attached it to the top immediately above the windshield. At the same time that the sunvisors were modified in early 1968, the mirror was changed to a break-away type mounted in the same area as before. It was molded from silver plastic as in contrast to its chrome plated predecessor.

The mirror used in 1969 and 1970 mounted on the windshield via an adhesive pad. It was modified in

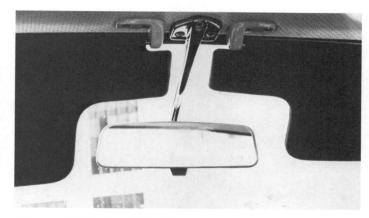

Mirror 1965-67 911/912

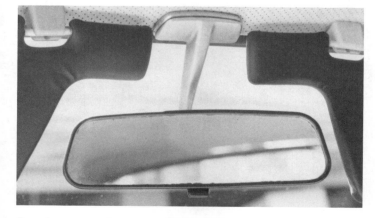

Break-away mirror on 1968 911

Mirror, 1969-70 mounted to the windshield

Mirror, 1971-73 was similar to its predecessor

1971 then remained unchanged through 1973. All rear view mirrors were of the day/night variety.

Upholstery

This topic is supplemented in the appendices section (page 94) regarding standard color combinations. This area may be slightly controversial as Porsche was known to build-to-order using special paints and upholstery as the customer wished. To detail these special combinations serves little purpose, not to mention being nearly impossible to research. The items covered in this section will be rear side walls, the rear seats and the rear compartment wall. The door panels will be discussed in the section on door hardware and the front seats in the section which follows this one.

The rear side wall is the upholstered panel behind the door panel. Like the door panel, it was capped by a separate trim panel. Since coupes and Targas differed substantially in this area, the rear side walls were never a shared item. The SWB 911 and 912 were all the same except color. The coupe version featured a seam around the the wheel well area. This was not the case on Targa models.

For 1969 through 1971 models these panels were

Rear compartment wall and rear side wall, 1966 911. Black washer is seat belt mounting location

Rear compartment wall, 1972 911

Revised location for shoulder harness mount, 1968

Side wall in 1972-73 had a compartment for the inertia reel seat belt

SWB Targa side upholstery, note long rear seat strap and that inner wheel arch is carpet rather than vinyl

changed, reflecting the modification in this area caused by the alteration of wheelbase. Coupe and Targa again differed.

The inertia reel seat belts first fitted in 1972 set U.S. specification coupes apart from those destined for the rest of the world. 1973 changed once again, although there is no obvious external difference. In 1973 Targas did not change; nor were U.S. models different from others. On Carrera models this panel was carpeted as an option.

Rear compartment area 1973 Targa

Rear seat area 1965-66 911. Note unique cushions

Rear seat area, 1973 Targa

Rear seat area, 1966 912

Rear seat strap, 1965 911

Rear seat area with vestigial seat belts, 1969

Luggage deposit. Optional from 1967 through 1971

The rear seats on the 1965-66 911s featured an upholstered area around the perimeter of the cushion, which was replaced by carpeting on later models and 912s. The seat backs on Targas were shorter than those on coupes, although the cushions were the same. There was no change in seat back and cushion from 1967 through 1971. Changes are noted for both 1972 and 1973. These were related to the different upholstery material used.

To hold the rear seat back in the "up" position, leather straps were fitted to the carpeted side of the seat. They were always black leather and had a metal snap which could be attached to the rear compartment wall. On SWB cars coupe and Targa models differed in length. The Targa ones were much longer (approximately 7 1/2 inches, compared to a little over 4 inches on coupes). The same ones were used through 1971 with a third variety used on 1971 911S models. For

1972 and 1973 a new strap was used. For the first time coupe and Targa shared the same strap.

An interesting substitute for the rear seats was offered on certain models from 1967 through 1971. In 1967 a "luggage deposit" was offered as an option on Targas. It featured two compartments in about the same location as the rear seat cushions. The access doors faced forward. The top of this compartment was a flat surface which was carpeted. The one used in 1968 was identical. The 1969 and 1970 model years had this option for both coupes and Targas. The last year it was offered was 1971 and by that time it had reverted to being only for Targas again and was the same one used in 1969 and 1970.

The rear compartment wall was the rear most upholstered panel in Porsche 911s and 912s. The panel used in coupes was always different from the one used on Targas due to the substantial difference in this area. The first change in the coupe rear panel was at chassis 308 091, 355 463 and 462 712 which corresponds to mid-1967. There were no additional changes to SWB cars. All SWB Targas used the same panel, differing only in color (see photos page 62).

These panels changed for all models in 1969. Coupes remained the same from 1969 through 1971 as did Targas. There was a difference between soft and fixed window Targas. 1972 brought a new rear panel. First the standard version featured a new upholstery fabric. U.S. specification cars were different from other models. For 1973 there was again another version, however, this time there was no U.S. type, per se. There were a couple of interesting alternatives in 1973. One was a rear shelf, which contained speakers for the radio. The other was an optional carpeted panel for the Carrera.

There is no mention of leather as an option for any of the aforementioned upholstery panels. This is not to say that they were not supplied. Full leather is listed as a 1965 through 1967 option, but disappears in 1968 (due to weird door panels probably) and makes a comeback in 1969 through 1973.

Seats

The seats in the first 911 and 912 cars were reminiscent of those found in 356 Porsches. They are not interchangeable, however, since the adjustment rails are farther apart on the 900 series. Nearly all were leatherette (vinyl), and all cars fitted with standard seats had chromed recliners on each side. Front to back adjusters were located on the side closest to the door below the seat.

The first seat style was used through chassis number

Early 911/912 seats looked suspiciously like 356 seats

Basket weave vinyl inserts on 1965 911 seats

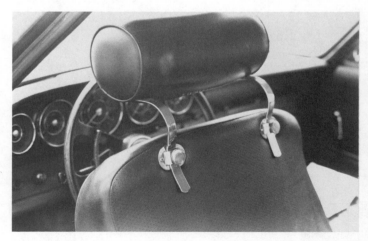

356 headrests were optional on 911/912s from 1965-1967

301 045 in 911s and 350 045 and 450 208 in 912s. This corresponds to an early 1965 change. No leather seat option is listed for this type seat. The next variety seat was used from this point until 12/31/67. Leather is listed as an option for this second type. U.S.-specification cars and RHD cars differed in that they had a locking seat back mechanism on the driver's seat. Headrests for these two seats were optional; the

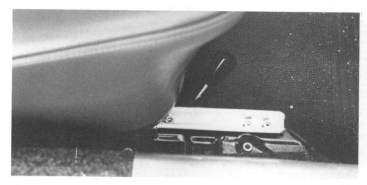

Fore/aft adjuster on early 911/912 seats

644 part number identifies these as being the same ones used on 356 models. They mounted on the upper rear of the seat back.

Cars built from 1/2/68 through the duration of the 1968 model year differed from their predecessors by having either a head rest installed or two little plastic plugs covering the holes where the head rest would have mounted. Head rests, like seats, could be upholstered in vinyl or leather. They could be adjusted for height and angle.

Seats used from 1969 through 1971 were similar in appearance to the earlier type with subtle changes in recliners and rails. Again, head rests were optional, the same ones used in 1968.

Different vinyl, recliners and inertia-type seat belts for 1972 and 73

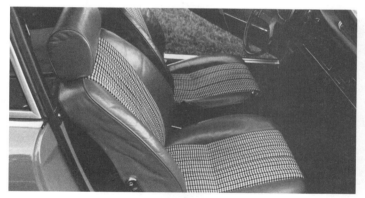

Hound's tooth cloth seat inserts, 1969 911. Note headrests and revised recliners with back release

Corduroy seat inserts. Note non-retracting seat belts doing what they did best. . becoming tangled

Recliner for 1972-73. Lever at top is the back lock release. Lower lever allows seat to recline. On the knob is the word Recaro

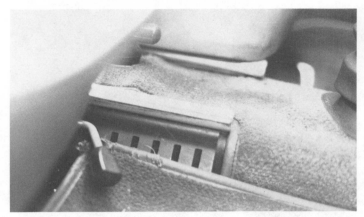

Fore/aft adjustment lever by 1972 had moved to the inside rail

Things grew slightly more complicated toward the end of this time period. In 1972, the side recliners went from chrome to black, and the vinyl used was slightly altered. For the first time, U.S. and European cars were the same, but that was not to last. In 1973 the rail mechanism was altered by adding a longitudinal adjustment lock. Once again, U.S. versions were different, this time due to the addition of a seat belt buzzer electrical connection. Vinyl and leather alternatives were again offered.

Sport seats were always available as optional equipment. For 1965 and 1966 there were two alternatives designated as "Recaro" and "Ferrari". Both were available in leather or vinyl with differing versions for 911 and 912 models.

There was only a single sport seat style for 1967 and 1968. It was made by Recaro, which incidentally made all of the standard seats as well. It was a reclining seat with substantial side bolsters. They were available in all leather, all vinyl or vinyl with inserts of corduroy or hound's tooth checked cloth. They were mounted on a steel hinging platform which allowed the seat to tilt forward, as well as slide back and forth. In 1968 they were not available on U.S. models.

1965-66 non-reclining "Recaro" sport seat

By 1969 sport seats became more civilized by adding adjustments both front to back and for height and pitch. Leather and vinyl were again available, and presumably cloth was also offered. The same sport seat was used from 1969 through 1971 being optional on all models and standard equipment on the 1971 911S. Both U.S. and European cars utilized a single type.

For 1972 and 1973, there was a different version for U.S. specification cars due to seat belt warning connections. Vinyl and leather were again offered.

The "Ferrari" seat bore more than a little resemblance to the Speedster seat of the 1950s

Sports seats, 1973. Note standard headrests were used after 1969

Reclining Recaro sport seat from 1967 did not incorporate a headrest

Seat rails were steel channels mounted on pressed steel brackets. There were two varieties of these brackets on SWB cars. One was for normal configuration and one for "raised" seats for those people who had trouble peering over the dash top. This option was not offered on 1969 and later cars. The rails on 1969 through 1972 cars were similar to the earlier cars and the ones on 1973 cars had the longitudinal adjustment lock mentioned previously.

Door-Related Items

This section will include the following items: door panels, arm rests, storage pockets, window cranks, electric window switches and lock knobs.

The door panels utilized in early 911 and 912 models featured a pleated pocket at the bottom. The first variety of door panel was used until the end of the 1966 model year. They were also used on 911S models up to chassis numbers 308 454S and 500 700S, which corresponds to a late 1967 change. A second type was used for other 1967 models up through chassis numbers 308 454 and 500 700 as well as 1965 through 1967 912s. The main difference in these two door panel styles is the rear of the lower pleated pocket. A stiff cardboard for on the earlier panel holds the rear portion permanently open.

Following this were the two final SWB versions of

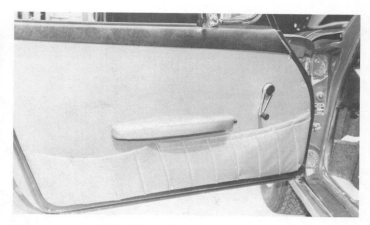

Door panel 1966 911. Note top is black. Rear pocket has fiberboard stiffeneing panel. No grab handle on driver's door

912 door panel did not have fiberboard insert in rear pocket. Grab handle was incorporated into passenger side arm rest

1967 911S, note aluminum trim below door top and cap on forward end of arm rest

door panel which were quite different in appearance. One style was used on 911S and 911L models with the other style used on the remaining 911s and 912s. Up to and including this panel, leather is not listed as being optional in the parts manuals, but it was in the 1965-1967 accessories manuals.

1969 through 1971 models with manually cranked windows shared the same door panel, which now had pockets that were not an integral part of the door panel.

The unique 1968 door panel. Note change in door top and pocket under arm rest. This European-spec. car does not have plastic covered vent handle. Speaker is not original

The 1971 cars with electric windows differed from the 1969 and 1970 cars by the brackets in which the switches were mounted. There were eight basic types of door panel. There were vinyl covered versions for those models with manual and electric windows and similar leather ones. In addition to these four, were four others for RHD cars. The RHD cars were different due to arm rest differences which will be described next.

Passenger side door panel 1969-71. Note revised arm rest and lower pockets. Basket weave material matched lower dashboard trim.

In 1972 there was a change in material but no substantial alteration in configuration. 1973 was again different. Like the 1969 through 1971 door panels, there were eight types. A ninth type was listed for 1973 Carrera. There was little information in the parts book about this, only that it was optional and only came in black. Due to the fact that it utilized a different handle, it was likely for weight saving. For all years, coupes and Targa models shared the same door panels.

The arm rest on all SWB cars was an upholstered rectangular device with a plastic push button on the

1972-73 door panel. No grab handle on driver's side

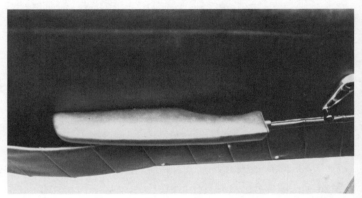

SWB arm rest. The little button at the front opened the door

forward end which unlatched the door. The inconspicuous nature of this button no doubt caused frequent panic from new owners and their passengers. The arm rest on the driver's side did not have a grab handle attached, since as we all know, both of the driver's hands were thought to be better placed on the steering wheel. Passengers, on the other hand, quite likely would need one, so it was provided. Leather and vinyl were available except on RHD cars, where leather was not available. The color of the arm rest matched the door panel unlike the door tops, which were always black through the 1966 model year. An aluminum cap adorned the forward end of the arm rest on the 1967 911S model, which also had a thin aluminum trim rail at the base of the interior door top.

The arm rest used from 1969 through 1973 was of the same material as the dash top. They were always black. The inner door handle was recessed into the arm rest and was not quite as subtle as the previous version. Grab handles followed the pattern previously established; however, they were not a separate piece as before. A different handle arrangement was available on the optional light-weight Carrera door panel.

The storage pockets on all SWB cars were upholstered and an integral part of the door panel. The ones on 1968 cars were substantially different than those

68

that came before. They were a formed, sealed vinyl covered cardboard pocket which spanned only the length of the arm rest. They were held "in" at the top by two elastic straps. In 1969, two pockets appeared at the bottom of the door panel. The front one was vinyl-covered fiberboard with an aluminum and rubber upper rim. The rear compartment was hinged at the base and was bordered at the top by the bottom of the arm rest. Construction was again vinyl covered fiberboard edged with aluminum trim. The inside of the compartments were flocked. The choice of fiberboard led to a number of problems associated with water damage which caused warping.

Electric windows were not offered on SWB cars, so all pre-1969 cars featured chrome window cranks. The earliest type had a black hard plastic knob and at the hub a small round vinyl cover concealed the mounting screw. This crank was used through the end of the 1966 model year. A second variety was introduced for 1967. It was similar in appearance and used the same vinyl cover. Between this cover and the knob was an arrow shaped vinyl cover. The final style of window crank was introduced just after the start of the 1968 model year at chassis numbers: 11 800 148, 11 820 005, 11 830 004, 11 850 036, 11 860 038, 11 805 001, 11 855 002, 11 870 001, 11 880 002, 12 820 031 and 12 800 240. Like the previous types this was a chrome handle of approximately the same size and shape. A soft vinyl knob replaced the hard plastic one and a grainy surfaced cover replaced the two vinyl pieces found on the previous edition. No additional changes were made through 1973.

Early uncovered vent handle and hard plastic lock knob

U.S.-spec. cars for the 1968 model year got soft vinyl lock knobs and vinyl covered vent window knobs

The early cars' interior lock knobs were hard plastic. They were replaced by a soft vinyl version with a rounded top. This was a 1968 model year change. There were no additional changes.

Threshold

Items covered in this section are heater slides, threshold rails, door seals, striker plates and door stays.

Heater slides were found on all SWB cars on the inside threshold in front of the seat. They were zinc-plated steel with a plastic slide. Appearance was nearly identical to those found on late model 356s; however, the mounting was with two screws as opposed to six on the 356.

Threshold rails used up through 1966 were polished stainless steel. They covered the edge of the carpet on the inside and held the lower part of the door seal on the outside. Starting with the 1967 model year and continuing through the end of 1973 a dull-finished aluminum rail replaced the stainless type.

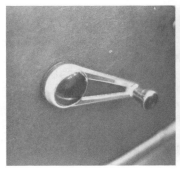

1965-66 window crank with hard plastic knob

Soft knob on late style window crank with grainy surfaced cover.

The electric window switches used from 1969 through 1972 were the same ones used for electric sunroof. There were two switches on the driver's side door panel and one on the passenger's side. Starting in 1971 a special mounting bracket in which the switches were housed was installed on each door panel. While this bracket remained unchanged through 1973, the switches were altered for the 1973 model year.

Heater slide was mounted at the front threshold. Aluminum carpet protector above is not original

Threshold area SWB. Standard rubber mat and stainless steel carpet rail

1967 911S with "S-trim" threshold. Ribbed aluminum threshold and carpet rail

A rubber mat covered the threshold outside the inner rail. On the 1967 911S and 1968 911S and 911L models (optional), this was replaced by ones that were dull ribbed aluminum. For 1969 through 1971 the aluminum mats were standard equipment on 911E and 911S models and optional (S-trim option) on other models. The rubber type came standard on these cars. In 1972 and 1973 the 911S and Carrera had the aluminum mats standard while they were optional on 911T and 911E.

The door seals on the earliest 911 and 912 models were reminiscent of those used on the 356 model; fitting in the channel provided and having an inner lip which overlapped the upholstery panels. These were used up to chassis number 301 124 which corresponded to an early 1965 change. The version used on Targas was identical in cross section but only fit around the front, back and bottom of the door. This Targa door seal was used from 1967 through 1973. The one used on coupes was changed in 1969 and again in 1972. They were redesigned in an attempt to lessen wind noise, which intensified as the seals deteriorated.

Early 1965

1965-68

1969-71

1972-73

The four different 911/912 door seal cross sections

Striker plates changed four times during this period. The original version was used through the end of the 1966 model year. It was improved for 1967 and 1968, although it retained the general appearance. A significant change occurred in 1969. This striker plate was used from that year through the 1972 model year. A final change was noted for 1973, although there is no obvious difference.

1965-66 style striker plate

Striker plates from 1967-on looked essentially like this

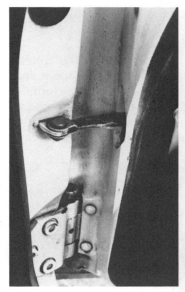

Door stay mechanism on SWB car

Door stay 1969-72. Note also paint plate and interior light switch

Door stay and hinge post area 1973

Chassis # 300 149 shows a unique fuel filler release mechanism. Note also uncovered light switch

release. In the first version of the owner's manual shows a knob above the top hinge. This feature was short lived. Soon into production the version below left was introduced as a stop-gap measure until the cable tube was rerouted. By early 1965 the knob took its familiar location to the left of the instrument pod.

Headliner

The headliner for coupes was light grey perforated vinyl with the windshield frame and B-pillar covered by non-perforated black vinyl.

All SWB cars used the same headliner except 1968 911L and 911S. There was, of course, a separate type installed on cars fitted with sunroofs. There were changes in 1969 when the color changed to beige and in 1973. A black perforated vinyl headliner was optional on 1973 Carreras. Headliners on Targas are discussed on page 7.

Interior lights on all coupes from 1964 through 1973 were the same. They mounted in the headliner above the B-pillar and were switched on, off or on when the door was opened by "rocking" the light on the wide axis. 1967 through 1973 Targas featured interior lights in the Targa bar. SWB cars used twin coupe lights mounted behind the side window. LWB cars had an air exhaust vent in this area so a single light was relocated to the top of the bar. These were mounted in vertical orientation and rocked along the narrow axis.

1965-67 interior light and rubber cloak peg

The door stay was a device intended to prevent the door from being opened farther than intended. It was mounted on the front of the door between the hinges. All SWB cars used the same one. It was modified in 1969 and the final time in 1973.

Also on the hinge post are the paint plate and interior light switch. On early cars there was no cover over the switch, but by mid-1966 they appeared.

One final feature on the first cars produced was the presence of the fuel filler

Cloak pegs (coat hooks) were mounted behind the interior lights and were again leftover 356 parts. The original version was tan rubber. For the 1968 model year it became black vinyl. In 1969 two separate cloak pegs were listed for use on coupe and Targa models (no peg was found on SWB Targas). The coupe peg was the one used in 1968. No additional changes were made through 1973.

SWB Targa interior light

LWB interior light mounted in the top of the Targa rollbar and pivoted on the narrow axis

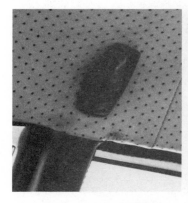 

Cloak peg used 1968-73 coupes and late Targas   *A slightly smaller cloak peg was listed for 1969 Targas*

Pedals and Levers

Only one fundamental change occurred in the foot pedal system. This was the addition of a bracket which held the warning light switch on the brake pedal for the 1968 model year. The brake and clutch pedal

pads were again renumbered 356 parts dating back to 1953.

The RHD configuration was substantially different than the LHD style (photo page 46). There were also left and right-hand drive versions of the Sportomatic pedal assembly, which was devoid of clutch pedal. The brake pedal pad on these cars was much larger than those with manual transmissions.

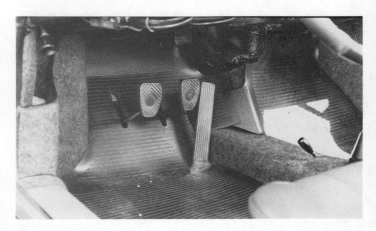

Manual transmission pedal assembly, 1967 912. Note rubber mats and Perlon carpet

The two pedal Sportomatic. Note narrow footwell of the Targa was due to strengthening panels

In the area between the seats was found the shift lever, the hand brake and the heater control and hand throttle levers.

The shift lever on the first cars was threaded for the plain black plastic screw-on shift knob. These were used through 1967. The first cars produced featured the mushroom shaped shift knob, as used on the 356B and 356C models (photo page 51). By the 1966 model year a round topped shift knob appeared. In 1968 a new type shift lever was used with a knob that pressed on to a fitting on the end of the shift lever. The knob used was black plastic with a clear portion on the top which revealed the shift pattern below. There was a different one for four and five-speed, as well as Sportomatic. The Sportomatic lever was considerably different due to the electrical micro switch which disen-

Early 911 leather shift boot

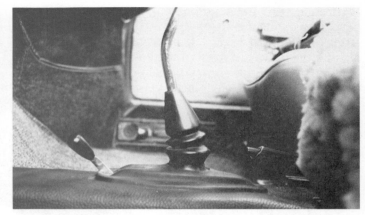

Rubber tunnel mat square-weave carpet, 1966 912

Round topped black plastic shift knob and top of rubber shift boot

Taller Sportomatic shift lever

Base of shift lever, heater control up front

five speed patterns. In 1973 the shifter mechanism was substantially modified. A boot, which was much larger covered this. The knobs were the same ones used in 1972.

Clear topped Sportomatic shift knob

gaged the clutch at the base. Shift boots on 1965 911s were leather, while 912s of the same vintage and later 911s had the same rubber boot that was found on 356B and 356C models.

1969 through 1971 used a different shift lever, although the appearance was similar. The same shift knobs and shift boot from the previous type were used. For 1972 the boot remained the same, but the remainder of the shift mechanism was different due to the 915 transmission, which had a revised shift pattern with reverse gear moving from the left to the right side. This necessitated a change in knobs for both four and

1973 shift lever with new larger boot. Cracked shift knob shows reverse below 5th gear

Through 1967 the hand brake mechanism did not incorporate the heat control lever. In these cars, it was in front of the shift lever. It operated by opening and closing the valves in front of the engine which directed heat into the interior compartment or let it escape under the car. The knob was black, yet another former 356 part.

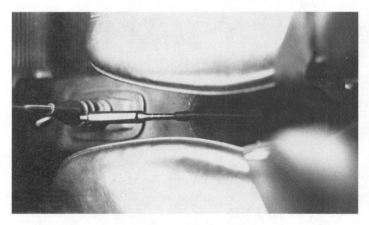

Handbrake assembly, through 1967

In 1968 the heat control lever moved behind the hand brake handle. It was located on the right side. On the left side was the hand throttle lever. It was capped by a round black knob. The heater knob was elongated and red in color. This hand brake assembly was used through 1971. For 1972 and 1973 the same basic configuration was used although heat and hand throttle control levers were different for U.S. and European cars.

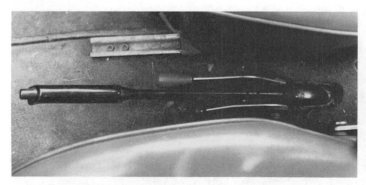

Hand brake assembly 1968-71, heat control on right, hand throttle on left

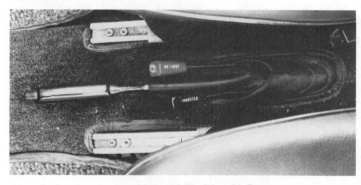

Hand brake assembly, 1972-73, U.S.-spec.

Carpet

The interior carpeting went through several changes. In both 911 and 912 manuals, rubber floor mats are listed for SWB cars. In fact, in the 912 manual the only carpeting for the front floor area is for RHD cars. The listing for rubber mats front and rear was confined to LHD 912 and down-market 911s, not including 911L and 911S models. By 1969, there were no more rubber mats.

For 911s a velour carpet was used through the end of 1966. This same carpet was used on early 1967 911S models through chassis numbers: 308 090 and 500 464. The carpet found in 912s of the same vintage was the same wool square weave that was used in 356 cars. According to information provided in the parts manuals, and all these carpets were charcoal grey.

In 1967 grey continued standard fare, although the material changed on the 912 and lesser 911 models. It now became the Perlon material described in the luggage compartment section on page 42. 911S and later 911L models continued to use the earlier velour. Colors other than grey were introduced at chassis numbers 308 091, 355 463, 462 712, 500 465 and 550 326, which corresponds to mid-year 1967 (see appendicies for colors, page 92).

For 1969 through 1971, 911E and 911S models came standard with velour carpeting, while 911T and 912s had Perlon. The 911T and 911E in 1972 and 1973 also came standard with Perlon, while 911S and Carrera were fitted with velour.

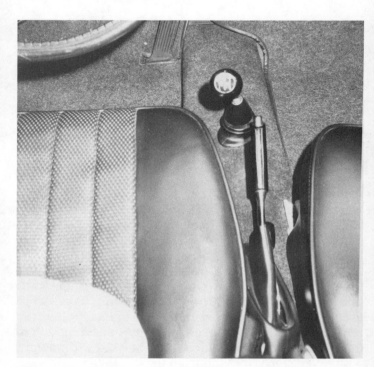

1969 911, Perlon carpet with no heel pads

APPENDICIES

Year Mfg.	Year Model	Official Model Design.	Engine Designation Official	Engine Designation Internal	Displ. cc.	Horse-power (DIN)-RPM	Stroke & Bore	Compr. Ratio
from Sep. '64	1965	911	2000	901/01	1991	130@6100	66/80	9.0:1
1965	1965 from Jan to Jun	911	2000	901/01	1991	130@6100	66/80	9.0:1
	1966 from Jul to Dec	912	912	616/36	1582	90@5800	74/82.5	9.3:1
1966	1966	911	2000	901/01	1991	130@6100	66/80	9.0:1
		911	2000	901/05	1991	130@6100	66/80	9.0:1
		912	912	616/36	1582	90@5800	74/82.5	9.3:1
	1967	911	2000	901/05	1991	130@6100	66/80	9.0:1
		911	2000	901/06	1991	130@6100	66/80	9.0:1
		911S	2000 S	901/02	1991	160@6600	66/80	9.8:1
		912	912	616/36	1582	90@5800	74/82.5	9.3:1
1967	1967	911	2000	901/06	1991	130@6100	66/80	9.0:1
		911S	2000 S	901/02	1991	160@6600	66/80	9.8:1
		912	912	616/36	1582	90@5800	74/82.5	9.3:1
1968	1968	911 USA	2000	901/14	1991	130@6100	66/80	9.0:1
		911 USA	2000	901/17	1991	130@6100	66/80	9.0:1

Carburetor (S) Solex (W) Weber (Z) Zenith	Engine Serial # I=Int. Heat E=Ext. Heat	Transm. Type (Standard)	Chassis Serial Numbers P = Porsche K = Karmann			Remarks
			Coupe (K)	Coupe (P)	Targa	
(S) 40 PI	900 001-900 360	901/0		300 001-300 235		901/0 Transm. series to Jul 65
(S) 40 PI	900 361-903 550	902/1		300 236-303 390		
(S) 40 PII-4	E 740 001-744 210 I 830 001-832 090	902/1* 902/0 USA	450 001-454 470	350 001-351 970		* from 66 model 902/1 transm. (5 sp) std except US
(S) 40 PI	903 551-907 000	902/1		303 391-305 100		
(W) 40 IDA 3 C, - 3 C 1	907 001-909 000	902/1				
(S) 40 PII-4	E 744 211-705 001 I 832 091-836 000	902/1 902/0 USA	454 470-458 100	351 971-353 000		
(W) 40 IDA 3 C, - 3 C 1	909 001-911 000	902/1 902/0 USA		305 101-307 350		
(W) 40 IDA 3 C, - 3 C 1	911 001-911 190	902/1 902/0 USA				
(W) 40 IDS 3 C, - 3 C 1	960 001-961 140	901/02		305 101 S-307 360 S		
(S) 40 PII-4	E 750 001-753 430 I 836 001-836 610	902/0 USA 902/1	458 101-461 140	354 001-354 970		
(W) 40 IDA 3 C, - 3 C 1	911 191-912 050	902/1 902/0 USA		307 351-308 522	500 001-500 718	4 sp. transm. for US
(W) 40 IDS 3 C, - 3 C 1	961 141-962 178	901/02		307 361 S-308 523 S	500 001S-500 718 S	
(S) 40 PII-4	E 753 431-756 195 I 836 611-837 070	902/1 902/0 USA	461 141-463 204	354 971-355 601	550 001-550 544	
(W) 40 IDAP 3 C, - 3 C 1	3 280 001-	902/0 USA 902/1	11 835 001-	11 830 001-	11 880 001-	w/ emission control
(W) 40 IDAP 3 C, - 3 C 1	3 380 001-	905/00				w/ emission control & Sportomatic

Year Mfg.	Year Model	Official Model Design.	Engine Designation Official	Engine Designation Internal	Displ. cc.	Horse-power (DIN)-RPM	Stroke & Bore	Compr. Ratio
1968	1968	911L	2000	901/06	1991	130@ 6100	66/80	9.0:1
		911L	2000	901/07	1991	130@ 6100	66/80	9.0:1
		911T	2000 T	901/03	1991	110@ 5800	66/80	8.6:1
		911T	2000 T	901/13	1991	110@ 5800	66/80	8.6:1
		911S	2000 S	901/02	1991	160@ 6600	66/80	9.8:1
		911S	2000 S	901/06	1991	160@ 6600	66/80	9.8:1
		911L USA	2000	901/14	1991	130@ 6100	66/80	9.0:1
		911L USA	2000	901/17	1991	130@ 6100	66/80	9.0:1
		912	912	616/36	1582	90@ 5800	74/82.5	9.3:1
		912 USA	912	616/39	1582	90@ 5800	74/82.5	9.3:1
1968/ 1969	1969	911T	911T	901/03 901/13 Sporto 901/16 US 901/19 US Sporto	1991	110@ 5800	66/80	8.6:1
		911E	911E	901/09 901/11 Sporto	1991	140@ 6500	66/80	9.1:1
		911S	911S	901/10	1991	170@ 6800	66/80	9.9:1

Carburetor (S) Solex (W) Weber (Z) Zenith	Engine Serial # I=Int. Heat E=Ext. Heat	Transm. Type (Standard)	Chassis Serial Numbers P = Porsche K = Karmann			Remarks
			Coupe (K)	Coupe (P)	Targa	
(W) 40 IDA 3 C, - 3 C 1	3 080 001-	902/1		11 810 001-	11 860 001-	
(W) 40 IDA 3 C, - 3 C 1	3 180 001-					w/Sportomatic
(W) 40 IDT 3 C, - 3 C 1	2 080 001-	901/10	11 825 001-	11 820 001-	11 870 001-	
(W) 40 IDT 3 C, - 3 C 1	2 180 001-					w/Sportomatic
(W) 40 IDS 3 C, - 3 C 1	4 080 001-	901/02		11 800 001-	11 850 001-	
(W) 40 IDS 3 C, - 3 C 1	4 180 001-	906/01				w/Sportomatic
(W) 40 IDAP 3 C, - 3 C 1	3 280 001-	902/0 (4 sp) 902/1 (5 sp)		11 805 001-	11 855 001-	w/emission control
(W) 40 IDAP 3 C, - 3 C 1	3 380 001-	906/00				w/emission control and Sportomatic
(S) 40 PII-4	I 1 080 001- E 1 085 001-	902/02	12 800 001-	12 820 001-	12 870 001-	
(S) 40 PII-4	1 280 001-	902/01				w/emission control
(W) 40 IDTP 3 C, - 3 C 1	619 0001- 619 2455 619 3001- 619 3297 619 5001- 619 7292 619 8001- 619 8184	901/06 or 901/12 905/13	119 10 0001- 119 10 0343	119 12 0001- 119 12 3561	119 11 0001- 119 11 1282	
			Chassis Number end December 1968			
			119 10 0131	119 12 1325	119 11 0247	
Fuel Injection	629 0001- 629 2270	901/07 or 901/13 901/06 USA 901/12 USA 905/13	119 20 0001- 119 20 0954	119 22 0001- 119 22 1014	119 21 0001- 119 21 0858	
			Chassis Number end December 1968			
	629 8001- 629 8583		119 20 0456	119 22 0329	119 21 0317	
Fuel Injection	639 0001- 639 2126	901/07 or 901/13	119 30 0001- 119 30 1492		119 31 0001- 119 31 0614	
			Chassis Number end December 1968			
			119 30 0586		119 31 0240	

| Year Mfg. | Year Model | Official Model Design. | Engine Designation | | Displ. cc. | Horse-power (DIN)- RPM | Stroke & Bore | Compr. Ratio |
			Official	Internal				
1968/ 1969	1969	912	912	616/36	1582	90@ 5800	74/82.5	9.3:1
		912 USA	912	616/40	1582	90@ 5800	74/82.5	9.3:1
1969/ 1970	1970	911T	911T-C	911/03 911/06 Sporto 911/07 US 911/08 US Sporto	2195	125@ 5800	66/84	8.6:1
		911E	911E-C	911/01 911/04 Sporto	2195	155@ 6200	66/84	9.1:1
		911S	911S-C	911/02	2195	180@ 6500	66/84	9.8:1
1970/ 1971	1971	911T	911T-C	911/03 911/06 Sporto 911/07 US 911/08 US Sporto	2195	125@ 5800	66/84	8.6:1
		911E	911E-C	911/01 911/04 Sporto	2195	155@ 6200	66/84	9.1:1
		911S	911S-C	911/02	2195	180@ 6500	66/84	9.8:1
1971/ 1972	1972	911T	911TV-E 911T-E	911/57 911/67 Sporto 911/51 US 911/61 US Sporto	2341	130@ 5600	70.4/84	7.5:1

Carburetor (S) Solex (W) Weber (Z) Zenith	Engine Serial # I=Int. Heat E=Ext. Heat	Transm. Type (Standard)	Chassis Serial Numbers P = Porsche K = Karmann			Remarks
			Coupe (K)	Coupe (P)	Targa	
(S) 40 PII-4	I 1 080 001- E 1 085 001-	902/04 or	129 00 0001-	129 02 0001-	129 01 0001-	
(S) 40 PII-4	1 280 001- 1 285 849	902/05 902/06	129 00 428 *above number incomplete*	129 02 3450	129 01 0801	
(Z) 40 TIN	610 0001- 610 3000 610 3501- 610 4547 610 3001- 610 3230 610 5001- 610 7999 610 8501- 610 9955 610 8001- 610 8374	911/00 905/20	911 010 0001- 911 010 2418 *Chassis Number end December 1969* 911 010 0793	911 012 0001- 911 012 4126 911 012 2275	911 011 0001- 911 011 2545 911 011 1089	
Fuel Injection	620 0001- 620 2478 620 8001- 620 8434	911/01 905/20	911 020 0001- 911 020 1304 *Chassis Number end December 1969* 911 020 0232	911 022 0001- 911 022 0667 911 022 0650	911 021 0001- 911 021 0933 911 021 0418	
Fuel Injection	630 0001- 630 2480	911/01	911 030 0001- 911 030 1744 *Chassis Number end December 1969* 911 030 0757		911 031 0001- 911 031 0729 911 031 0283	
(Z) 40 TIN or (W) 40 IDTP1	611 0001- 611 9001 611 4001- 611 9501-	911/00 905/20	911 110 0001- *Chassis Number end December 1970* 911 110 0977	911 112 0001- 911 112 1587	911 111 0001- 911 111 1523	
Fuel Injection	621 0001- 621 8001-	911/01 905/20	911 120 0001- *Chassis Number end December 1970* 911 120 0600		911 121 0001- 911 121 0456	
Fuel Injection	631 0001-	911/01	911 130 0001- *Chassis Number end December 1970* 911 130 0573		911 131 0001- 911 131 0389	
Carbuetor	652 0001- 652 3284 652 9001- 652 9224	915/12 905/21	911 250 0001- 911 250 1963 *Chassis Number end December 1971* 911 250 0781		911 251 0001- 911 251 1523 911 251 0687	
Fuel Injection	612 0001- 612 4478 612 9001- 612 9293	915/12 925/00	911 210 0001- 911 210 2931 *Chassis Number end December 1971* 911 210 1176		911 211 0001- 911 211 1821 911 211 0746	

Year Mfg.	Year Model	Official Model Design.	Engine Designation Official	Internal	Displ. cc.	Horse-power (DIN)-RPM	Stroke & Bore	Compr. Ratio
1971/ 1972	1972	911E	911E-E	911/52	2341	165@ 6200	70.4/84	8.0:1
				911/62 Sporto				
		911S	911S-E	911/53	2341	190@ 6500	70.4/84	8.5:1
				911/63 Sporto				
1972/ 1973	1973	911T	911TV-E	911/57	2341	130@ 5600	70.4/84	7.5:1
				911/67 Sporto				
			911T-E	911/51 US		140@ 5600		
				911/61 US Sporto				
				911/91 US		140@ 5700		8.0:1
				911/96 US Sporto				
		911E	911E-E	911/52	2341	165@ 6200	70.4/84	8.0:1
				911/62 Sporto				
		911S	911S-E	911/53	2341	190@ 6500	70.4/84	8.5:1
				911/63 Sporto				
		911SC	911SC-F	911/83	2687	210@ 6300	70.4/90	8.5:1

Carburetor (S) Solex (W) Weber (Z) Zenith	Engine Serial # I=Int. Heat E=Ext. Heat	Transm. Type (Standard)	Chassis Serial Numbers P = Porsche K = Karmann			Remarks
			Coupe (K)	Coupe (P)	Targa	
Fuel Injection	622 0001- 622 1765	915/12	911 220 0001- 911 220 1124		911 221 0001- 911 221 0861	
	622 9001- 622 9248	925/00	Chassis Number end December 1971 911 330 0378		911 221 0290	
Fuel Injection	631 0001- 632 2586	915/12	911 230 0001- 911 230 1750		911 231 0001- 911 231 0989	
	632 9001- 632 9147	925/01	Chassis Number end December 1971 911 230 0489		911 231 0311	
Carburetor	653 0001-	915/12	911 350 0001-		911 351 0001-	
	653 9001-	905/21	Chassis Number end December 1972 911 350 0834		911 351 0736	
Fuel Injection	613 0001-	915/12	911 310 0001- 911 310 1252		911 311 0001- 911 311 0781	
	613 9001-	925/00				
CIS	613 3001-	915/12	911 310 1501-		911 311 1001	
	613 9301-	925/00				
Fuel Injection	623 0001-	915/12	911 320 0001-		911 321 0001-	
	623 9001-	925/00	Chassis Number end December 1972 911 320 0584		911 321 0431	
Fuel Injection	633 0001-	915/12	911 330 0001-		911 331 0001-	
	633 9001-	925/01	Chassis Number end December 1972 911 330 0754		911 331 0468	
Fuel Injection	663 0001-	915/08	911 360 0001- Chassis Number end December 1972 911 360 0319			

SPOTTER'S GUIDE

FRONT

1964   Horn grilles mounted by four screws.
Hella 128 fog lights.
Covered sealed-beam headlights.
Silver wiper arms.
Bosch turnsignal units with unremovable lenses.
Chrome bumper guards.

1966 911

Mid - 1966   Horn grilles mounted by two screws.

1967   Optional rubber covered bumper guards.
Optional wide "S" bumper trim.

1968   Uncovered headlights with wide chrome rim.
Black wiper arms.

1968 911S

1969   Narrow chrome horn grilles.
Turnsignals with chrome trim and removable lens.
Optional Hella 169 fog lights.

1969 911T

1972   Optional black chrome bumper guards.
Optional 911S spoiler.

1973   Black, all rubber, bumper guards.
Black horn grilles.
Turnsignals with black trim.
Front mounted oil cooler with special bumper on Carrera

1973 911T

1964   Movable front vent windows.
Small door handle with push button release.
No rocker panel trim
Chrome or painted, 4 1/2" x 15" steel wheels.
Small round Durant side mirror.

1965   Rocker panel trim.

1965 911

1966 912

1967   4 1/2" x 15" Fuchs alloy wheels.
Wide rocker trim on 911S.

1967 911S

1968   Chrome or painted, 5 1/2" x 15" steel wheels.
5 1/2" x 15" Fuchs alloy wheels.
Small side reflectors front and rear. (1968 U.S. models only)
Wide aluminum rocker panel trim on 911S.
Aluminum side window trim.
"Winged" door handle with push button release.
Large round Durant side mirror

1968 911L

1968 911L

1969   Small flares on front and rear wheel arches.
Fixed front vent windows on coupes.
Long wheel base.
"S" rocker panel trim optional all models.
Optional wheel arch molding.
Optional 5 1/2" x 15" cast aluminum wheels 911T.
5 1/2" x 14" Fuchs wheels 911E.
6" x 15" Fuchs wheels 911S.

SIDE		REAR	

SIDE

1970   Door handle with trigger release.

1972   Oil filler on right rear fender.
Rectangular side mirror.
Chrome wheels no longer fitted.

1972 911T

1973   Black trim on lights.
Larger rear flares on Carrera.
7" x 15" Fuchs wheels Carrera
(rear)

1973 911T

REAR

1964   Chrome bumper guards.
2 piece Porsche script.
Bosch tail light units with unremovable lenses.
No model designation (901).
Bar in center of opening below rear grille.

1965   Angled 911 or 912 script.

1966 912

1967   Individual P-O-R-S-C-H-E letters
in aluminum or gold on rear lid.
"Straight" model designation scripts
above Porsche letter set.
Provision for rear wiper on rear lid.
Optional rubber covered bumper
guards.
Soft window Targa introduced.
Wide 911S bumper trim introduced.

Mid-1967   Rear bar for "ram protection"

1967 912

87

1968	Optional "fixed" window Targa. No bar in center of opening below rear grille (mid-year).
1969	Removable lens tail lights with chrome trim. Rear grille with flat topped aluminum bars. Reflectors added to rear bumpers. 911S bumper trim optional on other models.
1970	2.2 litre decal on rear window.
1972	No decal on rear window. Black rear grille. 2.4 insignia on rear grille Black Porsche letter set and model designation. Optional black chrome bumper guards.
1973	Duck tail rear lid on Carrera. Black trim on tail lights. Black, all rubber, bumper guards.

1971   911T

1973   911   Carrera   RS

1964	Painted dashboard on 912. No model designation on glove box door (901). Wood dashboard trim on 911/901. Ashtray in dashboard. Optional wood steering wheel. 356 "mushroom" shift knob. Leather shift boot 911. Heat control lever mounted in front of shift lever. Rubber floor mats 912. Carpet floor mats 911. Push button door release. "Stiff backed" rear door pocket on 911 only Optional 356 style headrests which bolt to the seat back.
1965	Black dashboard 912 Five instruments optional on 912. Optional ambient temperature gauge. Model designation present on glove box door. Brushed aluminum dashboard trim on 912. Rubber floor mats, some 911s Optional "butterfly" horn ring.
1966	Wrap around kneeguard. Aluminum backing on wood dashboard trim. Rubber shift boot on 911. "Round" shift knob.
1967	Wood dashboard trim deleted. Basket weave vinyl dashboard trim on 911S. Brushed aluminum dashboard trim on 911 and 912. Five gauges standard on 912. Black and white sun visors on coupes. All black sun visors on Targas. Optional leather steering wheel. Perlon carpet for models other than 911S. Carpet floor mats in all 911s. Aluminum trim on door top and arm rest 911S. "Stiff backed" rear door pocket on 911S only. Two vinyl covers on window cranks.

INTERIOR

1968   Basket weave or "elephant hide" vinyl dashboard trim on all models.
Hard foam dash top rear with soft vinyl speaker area.
Rubber covered dashboard knobs.
Black/white gauges.
Rubber knobs on turnsignal and wiper switches.
Air conditioning first offered. One part unit with controls on left side.
Shift pattern on shift knob.
Hand throttle and heater control combined with handbrake unit.
Door panels with pockets under arm rest only.
Large grained window crank cover.
Black plastic cover on front vent window release.
Round top lock knob.
Seats with integral head rests or plastic buttons.
Black plastic cloak peg.
Breaak away rear view mirror.

1969   Hard foam dashboard top with separate speaker grille.
Rear view mirror mounted to wind shield by adhesive pad.
Lever type blower control mounted in dashboard center.
Ash tray located in center of knee guard

1969 cont.   Two piece air conditioner with one control on each half.
Wood steering wheel no longer offered.
Plastic covered horn ring.
Power windows first offered.
Large arm rest with vinyl covered pocket below.
Black plastic lock release on seat recliners.
Ambient temperature gauge no longer offered.
Single interior light on Targa.
Seat locks present on recliners.

1970   Push button 4-way flasher switch.

1971   Twist knob on glove box.

1972   Model designation deleted from glove box door.
New shift pattern on shift knobs.
Reverse on right side.
Black recliners on seats.
Inertia reel seat belts.

1973   Hard rubber "Ebonite" steering wheel replaced by "foamed" wheel as standard equipment.
Large round shift boot.

EXTERIOR COLORS

First a few words about Porsche paint and the numbering as it appears in the following charts. Nearly all cars produced by Porsche after the 1955 model year were finished in enamel paint, which was baked following application. An exception to this lies in the metallic paints used from 1966 through 1969, which were lacquer. A so-called "two coat process" enamel paint replaced this lacquer from 1970 through 1973.

The plate bearing the paint number is located on the left door hinge post. The code on it indicates the original color of the car. Up through 1971 this number matched the one found in the "Number" column below. In 1970 different numbers were used on coupes and Targas, with the number ending in "10" signifying Targa and the repeating number signifying coupe models (one exception was black,which used the same number for coupe and Targa). For 1972 and 1973 the code used on the chassis plate was the "internal" number as found in the "Code" column.

It is interesting, although not surprising, to note that multiple paint suppliers were used. Information about the paint supplier as well as the coachbuilder is also contained on the paint plate. The paint manufacturer is coded by an alphabetic letter on early cars and a number on later cars. The coachbuilder is named on the early cars and given a numeric code on the later cars. An example of this coding on a black 1972 911 would be as follows:

700 / 9 / 3

The 700 is the color code. The 9 is the coachbuilder and the 3 is the paint manufacturer. While I do not have the number codes for the paint suppliers the letter codes for the earlier cars were H = Herbol, G = Glasurit and L = Lechler.

One final note, the colors followed by an asterisk (*) are those that were available for the U.S. market. Custom paint was always an option ($100 in 1965). The colors listed for the 1965 model year are identical to those found on 356 models built in the same year.

1965

Color	Number	Code
Slate Gray	6401	615
Ruby Red	6402	015
Sky Blue	6403	314
Light Ivory	6404	131
Champagne Yellow	6405	111
Irish Green	6406	213
Signal Red	6407	016
Dolphin Grey	6410	610
Togo Brown	6411	413
Bali Blue	6412	313
Black	6413	700

1966 - 1967

Color	Number	Code
Slate Gray*	6601	615
Polo Red*	6602	012
Gulf Blue*	6603	315
Light-Ivory*	6604	131
Bahama Yellow*	6605	110
Irish Green*	6606	213
Sand Beige*	6607	510
Aga Blue*	6608	310
Black*	6609	700
Burgandy Red	30868	017
Maroon	30736	
Tangerine	P2002	018

	Number	Code
Metallic Dark Red	30847	020
Champagne Yellow	16153	111
Signal Yellow	R1007	114
Canary Yellow	R1012	115
Medium Ivory	17657	132
Lido Gold	17656	
Golden Green	62165	216
Signal Green	R6001	217
Leaf Green	62163	218
Metallic Dark Green	62109	221
Green Turquoise	R6016	220
Velvet Green	62162	
Sea Green	62164	
Crystal Blue	52254	320
Pastel Blue	R5012	321
Prussian Blue	R5009	
Metallic Blue	52300	322
Ultra Blue	R5013	323
Olive	62166	414
Sepia Brown	R8007	415
Cocoa Brown	80342	416
Stone Grey	75741	
Light Grey	75742	620
Cloudy Grey	R7030	621
Beige Grey	70192	622
Black	95043	700
Silver Metallic	96024	924

1968 - 1969

Color	Number	Code
Slate Gray*	6801	615
Polo Red*	6802	012
Ossi Blue*	6803	319
Light-Ivory*	6804	131
Bahama Yellow*	6805	110
Irish Green*	6806	213
Sand Beige*	6807	510
Burgundy Red*	6808	017
Tangerine*	6809	018
Medium Ivory	6821	132
Champagne Yellow	6822	111
Signal Yellow	6823	114
Canary Yellow	6824	115
Crystal Blue	6825	320
Pastel Blue	6826	321
Ultra Blue	6827	323
Golden Green	6828	216
Signal Green	6829	217
Leaf Green	6830	218
Turquoise Green	6831	220
White (Light) Grey	6832	620
Cloudy Grey	6833	621
Beige (Oxford) Grey	6834	622
Olive	6835	414
Sepia Brown	6836	415
Cocoa Brown	6837	416
Black	6838	700
Silver Metallic	6851	924
Metallic Dark Green	6852	219
Metallic Blue	6853	322
Metallic Dark Red	6854	020

1970

Color	Number Targa/Coupe	Code
Light-Ivory*	1110/1111	131
Signal Orange*	1410/1414	116
Irish Green*	1510/1515	213
Tangerine*	2310/2323	018
Conda Green*	2610/2626	222
Bahia Red*	1310/1313	022
Albert Blue*	1810/1818	325
Pastel Blue*	2010/2020	321
Burgandy*	2410/2424	017
Silver Metallic*	8010/8080	925
Metallic Blue*	8410/8484	324
Metallic Red*	8110/8181	021
Metallic Green*	8310/8383	221
Light Red	7910/7979	023
Signal Yellow	7210/7272	114
Canary Yellow	2910/2929	115
Light Yellow	6210/6262	117
Medium Ivory	4610/4646	132
Signal Green	7810/7878	217
Leaf Green	7710/7777	218
Turquoise Green	6510/6565	22

Color	Number	Code
Crystal Blue	7310/7373	320
Glacier Blue	6610/6666	326
Adriatic Blue	1610/1616	327
Turquoise	6410/6464	340
Olive	3910/3939	414
Sepia Brown	7410/7474	415
Light Grey	7610/7676	620
Beige (Oxford) Grey	7510/7575	622
Black	1010	700

1971

Color	Number Targa/Coupe	Code
Burgandy Red*	2410/2424	017
Tangerine*	2310/2323	018
Metallic Red*	8110/8181	021
Bahia Red*	1310/1313	022
Light Red	7910/7979	023
Signal Yellow	7210/7272	114
Signal Orange*	1410/1414	116
Light Yellow	6210/6262	117
Light Ivory*	1110/1111	131
Medium Ivory	4610/4646	132
Gold Metallic*	8810/8888	133
Irish Green*	1510/1515	213
Signal Green	7810/7878	217
Leaf Green	7710/7777	218
Green Turquoise	6510/6565	220
Metallic Green*	8310/8383	221
Conda Green*	2610/2626	222
Crystal Blue	7310/7373	320
Pastel Blue*	2010/2020	321
Metallic Blue*	8410/8484	324
Albert Blue*	1810/1818	325
Glacier Blue	6610/6666	326
Adriatic Blue	1610/1616	327
Gemini Blue Metallic*	8610/8686	330
Turquoise	6410/6464	340
Olive	3910/3939	414
Sepia Brown	7410/7474	415
White Grey	7610/7676	620
Beige Grey	7510/7575	622
Black	1010	700
Silver Metallic*		924
Silver Metallic (2-coat)*	8010/8080	925

1972

Color	Number Targa/Coupe	Code
Tangerine*	2310/2323	018
Gulf Orange	6110/6161	019
Bahia Red*	1310/1313	022
Rose Red (Raspberry)	3310/3333	024
Aubergine*	4010/4040	025
Signal Yellow*	7210/7272	114

1972

Color	Number Targa/Coupe	Code
Signal Orange	1410/1414	116
Light Yellow*	6210/6262	117
Light Ivory*	1110/1111	131
Ivory	4610/4646	132
Gold Metallic*	8810/8888	133
Irish Green	1510/1515	213
Leaf Green	7710/7777	218
Metallic Green*	8310/8383	224
Emerald (Kelly) Green	3810/3838	225
Lime Green (Chartreuse)	6710/6767	226
Jade (Light) Green	6810/6868	227
Metallic Blue*	8410/8484	324
Albert Blue*	1810/1818	325
Glacier Blue	6610/6666	326
Gulf Blue	3610/3636	328
Oxford (Dalmatian) Blue	3510/3535	329
Gemini Blue Metallic*	8610/8686	330
Royal Purple (Lilac)	6910/6969	341
Olive	3910/3939	414
Sepia Brown*	7410/7474	415
Beige Grey	7510/7575	622
Black*	1010	700
Silver Metallic*	8010/8080	925

1973

Color	Number Targa/Coupe	Code
Tangerine*	2310/2323	018
Gulf Orange	6110/6161	019
Bahia Red*	1310/1313	022
Rose Red (Raspberry)	4510/4545	024
Aubergine*	4010/4040	025
Guards Red	2510/2525	027
Signal Yellow*	5210/5252	114
Signal Orange	1410/1414	116
Light Yellow*	6210/6262	117
Light Ivory*	1110/1111	131
Ivory	4610/4646	132
Gold Metallic*	8810/8888	133
Irish Green	1510/1515	213
Leaf Green	5610/5656	218
Metallic Green*	8310/8383	224
Emerald (Kelly) Green	3810/3838	225
Lime Green (Chartreuse)	6710/6767	226
Jade Green	6810/6868	227
Metallic Blue*	8410/8484	324
Albert Blue	1810/1818	325
Glacier Blue	6610/6666	326
Gulf Blue	6010/6060	328
Oxford Blue (Dalmatian)	4810/4848	329
Gemini Blue Metallic*	8610/8686	330
Royal Purple (Lilac)	6910/6969	341
Olive	3910/3939	414
Sepia Brown*	5410/5454	415
Beige Grey	5510/5555	622
Black	1010	700
Silver Metallic*	8010/8080	925

INTERIOR COLOR COMBINATIONS

1965 - 1968

Upholstery Color
  Red
  Black
  Brown
  Beige
Upholstery Material
  Vinyl (standard)
  Leather (optional)
Seat Inlays
  Basket Weave Leatherette
    Red
    Black
    Brown
    Beige
  Hound's Tooth Cloth
    Black/Red/White
    Black/White
    Black/Brown/White
  Corduroy
    Red
    Black
    Cognac
    Stone-gray
Carpet
  "Black" (dark grey).

1969 - 1971

Upholstery Color
  Black
  Brown
  Beige
Upholstery Material
  Vinyl (standard)
  Leather (optional)
Seat Inlays
  Basket Weave Leatherette (or Leather)
    Black
    Brown
    Tan
  Hound's Tooth Cloth
    Black/White
    Black/Brown/White
  Corduroy
    Black
    Brown
    Tan
Carpet
  "Black" (dark grey) velour
  Brown Perlon
  Charcoal Perlon

1972 - 1973

Upholstery Color
  Black
  Brown
  Tan
  Blue (vinyl only)
  Red (vinyl only)
Upholstery Material
  Vinyl (standard)
  Leather (optional)
Seat Inlays
  Perforated Leatherette (or Leather)
    Black
    Brown
    Beige
  Hound's Tooth Cloth
    Black/White
    Black/Brown/White
  Corduroy
    Black
    Brown
    Tan
  Plaid Cloth (Madras)
    Orange
    Blue
    Tan
Carpet
  Black
  Charcoal
  Brown

For information on carpet material for these years, see page 74.

INDEX